The Genus *Paeonia*

The Genus *Paeonia*

Josef J. Halda

with notes on cultivation by

James W. Waddick

Botanical illustrations by Jarmila Haldová

Timber Press
Portland • Cambridge
in association with
the Heartland Peony Society

Published in 2004 by
Timber Press, Inc.   Timber Press
The Haseltine Building   2 Station Road
133 S.W. Second Avenue, Suite 450   Swavesey
Portland, Oregon 97204-3527, U.S.A.   Cambridge CB4 5QJ, U.K.

Printed in Hong Kong

Library of Congress Cataloging-in-Publication Data

Halda, Josef J.
      The genus Paeonia / Josef J. Halda ; with notes on cultivation
by James W. Waddick ; botanical illustrations by Jarmila Haldov.
            p.   cm.
      Includes bibliographical references and index.
      ISBN 0-88192-612-4
      1. Peonies. I. Waddick, James W. II. Title.
      SB413.P4 H24   2004
      635.9'33111–dc21
                                                2003013596

A catalog record for this book is also available from the British Library.

Publication of this volume
was made possible by the generous support of the
Heartland Peony Society,
whose mission is to foster an interest in peonies,
to promote their introduction into cultivation,
and to encourage development of new and improved varieties.

For further information, please contact

Heartland Peony Society
713 White Oak Lane
Gladstone, MO 64116-4607
TEL: 816-453-5387
WEB: www.peonies.org

Contents

PART II   GROWING PEONY SPECIES
James W. Waddick and Josef J. Halda

Preface and Acknowledgments
of Josef J. Halda

The first time I encountered wild peonies in bloom in nature was when I was six years old, in Dobruja, Romania. My father, a painter, loved the Black Sea coast, especially in the springtime, when entire hills are covered with flowers, including carmine clumps of *Paeonia tenuifolia*, creating an unforgettable picture. Later on, the yellow-flowered Caucasian peonies and the woody peonies of western China, which look like small miracles, enriched my life greatly.

Over the past thirty years, my wife, Jarmila, and I systematically observed and collected specimens and seeds of wild peonies, building collections of living plants and herbarium specimens that now comprise almost all the known species. We worked on this book for more than fifteen years, traveling around the world, collecting plants and seeds, examining many thousands of herbarium specimens, and documenting all the most interesting localities. Thus, all the color plates in this book were painted from living plants, mostly as watercolor sketches done on the site.

We are very grateful to the large number of friends who helped us in many ways. Of these, we particularly wish to mention Eona Aitken, Bonnie Brunkow, Phyllis Gustafson, Sean Hogan, Marcel Jouseau, Ida Kalinina, John Lavranos, Coleman Leuthy, Ron and Susan McBeath, Jiri Sojak, Jean Stevens, Irina Verescagina, and Michal Zaprjagaev.

Preface and Acknowledgments
of James W. Waddick

I came to this project relatively late in its life compared to the senior author's vast experience. I realize this is not a definitive work as more people grow more plants in more areas of the world. Much of this information has never been collected in one place. The color plates and line drawings make this book especially noteworthy. Names of species and higher taxonomic categories are open to differences of opinion, but their usage in Part II complies with Josef's conclusions in Part I. Conflicting views, especially of tree peony taxonomy, reflect all that is yet to be learned.

My contributions on cultivation are based on years of growing plants in the sometimes hard conditions of the American Midwest with unkind patterns of excesses: heat, cold, drought, wind, and more. I have also relied on comments from growers around the world and a community of commercial growers and enthusiastic backyard gardeners in the United States, Europe, and Australia.

Thanks go to many people, but a special thanks to the leadership of Al Rogers who started the current renewal of interest in all kinds of peonies. Thanks to Carsten Burkhardt, the late Leo Fernig, Wilbert Hetterscheid, Don and Lavon Hollingsworth, Bob Johnson, Irmtraud Rieck, Cyndi and Charlie Turnbow, and members of the electronic peony group. Thanks to Jerry Flintoff, Daniela Goll, and Francesca Thoolen for translation help. I am also pleased to have the support of a host of local peony lovers in the Heartland Peony Society especially their president, Claudia Schroer.

Thanks to Timber Press for supporting my involvement and for its kindness in putting up with the peculiar problems involved in making this book work: thanks, Neal.

I dedicate this book to Caitlin and Jim.

PART I

The Genus *Paeonia*

Josef J. Halda

Figure 1. *Paeonia* woodcut in *Herbolario volgare* published in Venice in 1522, probably *P. officinalis.*

CHAPTER 1

History of Peony Studies

The name *Paeonia* supposedly commemorates Paean or Paeon, whom Homer mentions as the physician of the Greek gods on Mount Olympus. After Homer's time the god Apollo assimilated the character of the physician Paeon, and the *paean* was a hymn of praise, originally dedicated to him. Apollo numbered medicine among the disciplines of which he was patron, and his epithet was applied to this group of plants because they were important in Greek medicine. An anonymous Greek bucolic poet of the third century C.E. praised the peony as the queen of herbs, and in China some centuries later, the shrubby moutan (*Paeonia suffruticosa*) became known as *hua wang*, the king of flowers.

An early discussion of the peony is found in the botanical treatises of Theophrastus (ca. 370–288 B.C.E.), who mentioned a superstition concerning the plant, which some people then called glukuside (glucoside in some English versions), from *glukus*, meaning "sweet, delightful." This plant, wrote Theophrastus (1916, 9: cap. 6), "should be dug up at night, for if a man does it in the daytime and is observed by a woodpecker, he risks the loss of his eyesight."

The Roman naturalist Pliny the Elder (1601, 7: 156–157) wrote about peonies:

> The first plant to be discovered was the peony, which still retains the name of the discoverer; it is called by some pentorobon, by others glycyside, for an added difficulty in botany is the variety of names given to the same plant in different districts. It grows on shaded mountains, having a stem among the leaves about four fingers high, which bears on its top four or five growths like almonds, in them being a large amount of seed, red and black. This plant also prevents the mocking delusions that the Fauns bring on us in our sleep. They recommend us to uproot it at nighttime, because the woodpecker of Mars, should he see the act, will attack the eyes in its defense.

This appears to be the only record of the woodpecker as a defender and conservationist of peonies, although the ancient Italians regarded it as a bird of prophecy, another realm sacred to Apollo.

Stearn and Davis (1984) remarked that certain Greek poems attributed to Hesiod (fl. ca. 800 B.C.E.) and Theocritus (ca. 310–250 B.C.E.) allude to a rivalry between the accomplished physician Paeon and his teacher Aesculapius, who jealously caused Paeon's death. Paeon had, however, cured Hades (god of the underworld) of an arrow wound, and the grateful Hades transformed him into the herb thereafter named *paeonia*. According to another myth, Leto, the mother of Apollo, revealed to Paeon that a herb growing on Mount Olympus could be used for easing childbirth, and this plant was later named *paeonia* for its first user.

The earliest surviving scientific account of peonies is in the herbal *De Materia Medica*, written in 77 C.E. by Greek physician Pedanios Dioscorides. He distinguished two kinds by their foliage: the "male peony" (*paionia arren*) and the "female peony" (*paionia theleia*). The male peony is said to have leaves like the walnut, that is, rather coarse, imparipinnate with distinct broad leaflets, and the female to have leaves like *Smyrnium*, that is, much more divided. Dioscorides was copied by scribes all through the Middle Ages in both the original Greek and the Latin versions, with the result that extant texts show much variation through the errors, rearrangements, and additions of the copyists and editors. Comparison of numerous manuscripts enabled Max Wellmann (1906, 2: 149–150) to establish what scholars now accept as the authentic Dioscoridean text:

> Paeonia or glycyside which some name pentorobon, dactylos idaeos, the root paeonia, others aglaophotida. The stem grows two [hand]spans high and has many branches. The male has leaves like walnut, the female much divided leaves like smyrnium. At the top of the stem it produces pods like almonds, in which when opened are found many small red grains like the seeds of pomegranate and in the middle five or six purplish black ones. The root of the male is about the thickness of a finger and a span long, with an astringent taste, white, the root of the female has seven or eight swellings like acorns as in asphodel. The dried root is given to women who have not been cleansed (internally) after childbirth. It promotes menstruation (a dose containing root the size of an almond being drunk); it lessens abdominal pains when drunk in wine. It helps those who have jaundice and kidney and bladder troubles. Soaked in wine and drunk, it stops diarrhea. Ten to twelve red grains from the fruit taken in dark rough (dry) wine stop menstrual flow and being eaten they ease stomach pains. Drunk and eaten by children, they remove the beginnings of stone. The black seeds are good against nightmares, hysteria, and pains of the womb when up to fifteen are drunk in mead of wine. It grows on high mountains and foothills.
>
> Male paeonia or glycyside, some name pentorobon, orobadion, orobax, haemagogon, pasidee, menogeneion, menion, paionion, Panos cerata, Idaeos dactylos, aglaophotida, theodoreton, selenion, selenogogon of the prophets, phthisis, the Romans casta. Female paeonia also called aglaophotida.

The medicinal use of peonies was long known to traditional physicians. Modern researchers have found that the roots of peonies (known to herbalists as *Radix Paeoniae*) contain peregrinin or paeonin, a substance formerly considered an alkaloid, but apparently a glycoside, which yields an oil known as paeonol. This oil has limited use even now in Asian medicine. Western naturopathic and homeopathic practitioners also used the flowers (*Flores Paeoniae*) and seeds (*Semen Paeoniae*).

The characteristics of the roots are described in detail by Hermann Thoms (1929) and in less detail by R. C. Wren in *Potter's New Cyclopaedia of Botanical Drugs and Preparations*. According to Wren (1968, p. 323),

The root appears in commerce in scraped, spindle-shaped pieces, averaging 3 inches [ca. 8 cm] long and 0.5–0.75 inches [12–20 mm] in diameter, pinkish gray or dirty white, strongly furrowed, and shrunken longitudinally. The transverse section is starchy, radiate with the medullary rays more or less tinged with purple.

In naturopathic beliefs, the peony retains its ancient reputation for having good antispasmodic and sedative properties, according to Wren and French author P. Fournier (1948). Like many other plants used for medicine, however, the peony is quite toxic; gardeners must be careful that children and domestic animals do not ingest any part of the plants.

Johannes P. de Lignamine in 1481 published *Herbarium Apulei Platonici* from a medieval manuscript, apparently of the ninth century, found in the library of the Montecassino abbey. In 1484 Peter Schoeffer in Mainz published the first German-printed herbal (which, having no printed title, is variously known as *Herbarius*, *Herbarius Moguntinus*, *Aggregator practicus de Simplicibus*, or the *Latin Herbarius*), with Latin text and woodcut illustrations supposedly

Figure 2. Woodcuts of *Paeonia officinalis* in (left) *German Herbarius* (Schoeffer 1485) and in (right) *Ortus Sanitatis*, published in Mainz in 1497.

derived from a 14th-century manuscript source; this work, however, contains no illustration of a peony. In 1485 Schoeffer published a much larger and differently illustrated herbal with German text, variously known as *Der Gart*, *Gart der Gesundheit*, *Herbarius zu Teutsch*, or *German Herbarius*.

Leonhart Fuchs (1501–1566), who from 1535 to 1566 was professor of medicine at the University of Tübingen, published his *De Historia Stirpium* (Treatise on Herbs) in Latin in 1542, and a German edition, *New Kreuterbuch* in 1543; both contain the same woodcut illustration of a peony (*Historia*, p. 202; *Kreuterbuch*, t. 112), hand-colored in some copies, under the names *Paeonia femina* ("female peony") and *Peonienbluom Gichtwurz* ("gout-root"). Fuchs stated that the peony was planted in all gardens in Germany. Carl Linnaeus cited this illustration as representing the species he named *Paeonia officinalis alfa feminea* ×*alfa* reflects a taxonomic system in use before the present one, in which the names of Greek letters were used to indicate what we

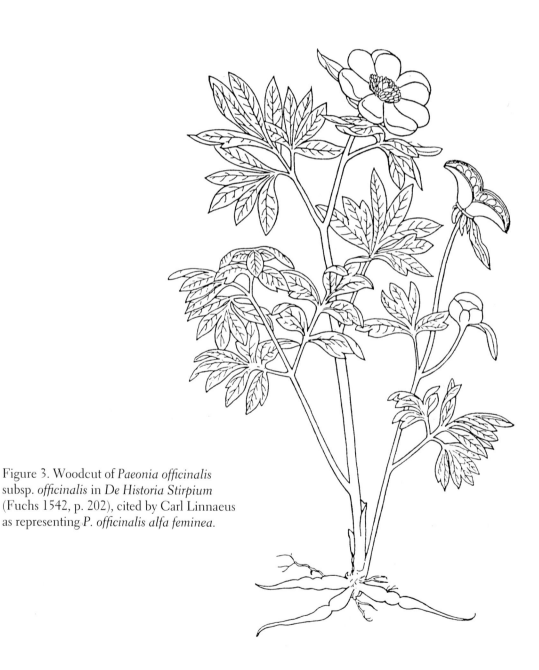

Figure 3. Woodcut of *Paeonia officinalis* subsp. *officinalis* in *De Historia Stirpium* (Fuchs 1542, p. 202), cited by Carl Linnaeus as representing *P. officinalis alfa feminea*.

now call varieties); this unambiguously established the specific name of the widely grown European species, with the word *officinalis* referring to the fact that it was used in medicine.

Pier Andrea Mattioli (Matthiolus, 1500–1577), physician to Roman emperor Rudolph II, wrote a herbal that was translated by Tadeas Hajek z Hajku and published in Czech in 1562 under the title *Herbarz, Jinak Bylinarz*. It contains an elaborate woodcut of the same species under the name *Paeonia*. Mattioli used the same illustration in his *Commentarii in sex libros Pedacii Dioscoridis* (1565), retitling it *P. foemina*. He added another woodcut under the name *P. mas*, which portrays the species now called *P. mascula*. Mattioli recorded *P. foemina* as common in Italy, but *P. mas* as found in only a few places. He made clear the differences between the roots of *P. officinalis* and *P. mascula*.

Matthias de l'Obel (Lobelius, 1538–1616) in *Plantarum seu stirpium icones* published illustrations of both *Paeonia officinalis* (as *P. femina*) and *P. mascula* (as *P. mas*).

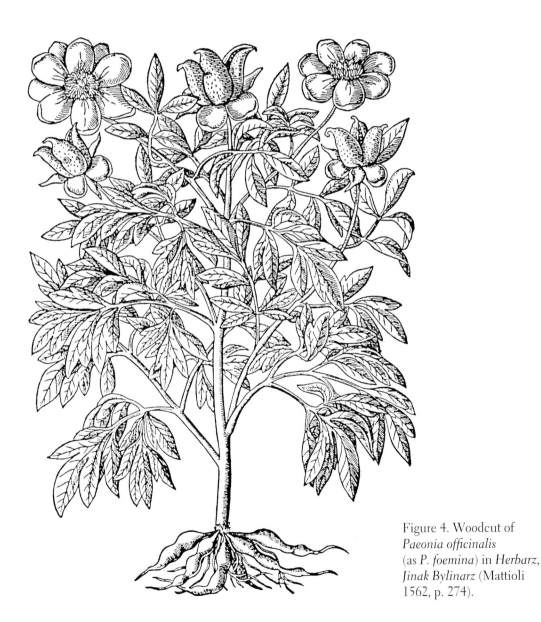

Figure 4. Woodcut of *Paeonia officinalis* (as *P. foemina*) in *Herbarz, Jinak Bylinarz* (Mattioli 1562, p. 274).

Figure 5. Woodcut of
Paeonia mascula subsp.
mascula (as *P. mas*) in
Commentarii (Mattioli
1565, p. 914).

Pierre Belon (1517–1564), a French naturalist who traveled in the Near East between 1546
and 1549, published *Les Observations de plusieurs singularités et choses memorables trouvées en
Grèce, Asie, Judée, Egypte, Arabie et autres pays estranges*. This work contains the first European record of a peony of Crete, probably *Paeonia clusii*.

Charles de l'Ecluse (Carolus Clusius, 1526–1609) in *Rariorum Plantarum Historia* (1601)
described several peonies. One, which he called *Paeonia cretica*, was later named *P. clusii* in his
honor; the other he called *P. byzantino semine nata*, now known as *P. peregrina*.

Caspar Bauhin's *Pinax Theatri botanici* (1623) portrayed five peonies: *Paeonia folio nigri-
cante splendido, quae mas*, the "peony with shining dark-tinted leaves, or male," now *P. mascula*
subsp. *mascula*; *P. communis vel foemina*, the "common or female peony," now *P. officinalis*
subsp. *officinalis*; *P. tenuis laciniata subtus pubescens flore purpureo*, the "slender peony with lacy
leaves, downy underneath, and purple flowers," now *P. officinalis* subsp. *humilis*; *P. folio subtus*

Figure 6. Woodcuts of *Paeonia officinalis* subsp. *officinalis* in *Plantarum* (l'Obel 1581, t. 830).

incano, flore albo vel pallido, the "peony with leaf white below, flower white or pale [pink]," now *P. clusii*; and *P. peregrina flore sature rubente*, the "wandering peony with flower fully red," now *P. peregrina*. The last species was also among the several peonies in Basilius Besler's *Hortus Eystettensis* published in 1613.

By the 18th century, European botanists were becoming cognizant of East Asian plants. Engelbert Kaempfer, in *Amoenitatum exoticarum* (1712, fascicle V), described herbaceous and shrubby peonies, both single and double, under the Japanese names *saku-jaku* (probably *Paeonia lactiflora*), *kamigusa*, and *hatskanguza* (*P. suffruticosa*).

In *Species Plantarum* (1753, 1: 530), the work that established the system of botanical nomenclature still in use today, Carolus Linnaeus (1707–1778) unified all the peonies known to him under one name, *Paeonia officinalis*, with two varieties, *feminea* and *mascula*. Linnaeus's single species embraced the plants now known as *P. officinalis*, *P. mascula*, and *P. clusii*.

Figure 7. Woodcuts of *Paeonia mascula* subsp. *mascula* in *Plantarum* (l'Obel 1581, t. 832).
Plant in flower and open follicle.

J. G. Gmelin, in *Flora Siberica* (1769, vol. 4), mentioned three species, later known as *Paeonia anomala*, *P. lactiflora*, and *P. tenuifolia*. By the time Philip Miller (1691–1771) published the 8th edition of his *Gardener's Dictionary*, he was able to mention six epithets for the genus *Paeonia*: *foemina*, *hirsuta*, *lusitanica*, *mascula*, *peregrina*, and *tatarica*. Peter S. Pallas in *Reise durch verschiedene Provinzen des russischen Reichs* (1776) described *P. anomala*, *P. hybrida*, *P. laciniata*, *P. lactiflora*, and *P. lobata*. Anders J. Retzius in *Observationes botanicae* (1783, vol. 3) mentioned *P. anomala*, *P. corallina*, *P. humilis*, and *P. officinalis*. Johannes Sebastian Mueller in *Illustratio Systematis Sexualis* (1777) published a picture of *P. officinalis* that we can now identify as *P. mascula*. Sibthorp and Smith in *Prodromus Flora Graeca* (1809, 1: 369–370) mentioned several Balkan species.

The first work devoted entirely to these plants was George Anderson's "A Monograph of the Genus *Paeonia*," which appeared in the taxonomic journal *Transactions of the Linnean Society*,

Figure 8. Woodcut of *Paeonia peregrina* in *Rariorum Plantarum* (Clusius 1601, 1: 281), the first illustration of this species.

London, in 1818. Anderson described several new species, including *P. arietina* and *P. decora*.

Pioneering botanists extended the range of the genus into the New World, and in *Flora Boreali-Americana* (1829) Sir William Hooker described *Paeonia brownii*. From the interior of Asia, John F. Royle (*Illustrations of the Botany of the Himalayan Mountains*, 1834) described *P. emodi*.

Camille Alexis Jordan (1814–1897) and Jules Fourreau (1844–1870) published several names in 1903, including *Paeonia glabrescens*, *P. leiocarpa*, *P. modesta* (synonym *P. officinalis* subsp. *humilis*), *P. monticola*, *P. revelieri* (synonym *P. mascula* subsp. *russoi*), and *P. villarsii* (synonym *P. officinalis* subsp. *officinalis*).

Adrien René Franchet worked on Abbé Delavay's collections from China. He described *Paeonia delavayi* and *P. lutea* in 1886.

Two monographs on the genus addressed 19th-century discoveries almost simultaneously. Ernst Huth (1845–1897) wrote "Monographie der Gattung *Paeonia*" in 1891. He combined many names assigned by earlier workers, treating them as subspecies or varieties of a small number of species. In 1890 R. Irwin Lynch published "A New Classification of the Genus *Paeonia*" in which he divided the genus into three subgenera: *Moutan*, *Onaepia*, and *Paeon*.

George L. Stebbins, Jr., published "Notes on Some Systematic Relationships in the Genus *Paeonia*" in 1939, with morphological notes of the sepals. Otto Stapf (1857–1933) worked on peonies but never published a revision.

Frederick Claude Stern (1884–1967), a famous peony grower and collector, published *A Study of the Genus* Paeonia (1946), a beautiful book with many splendid color plates, useful both for taxonomists and gardeners.

Recent works are few. Wen Pei Fang (1958) revised the Chinese species, adding several new descriptions. K. Y. Pan published a subsequent revision of the Chinese species in *Flora Reipublicae Sinicae* (1979). Russian botanist L. M. Kemularia-Nathadze (1961) addressed the Caucasian species of *Paeonia,* in which he described many new taxa, a practice typical of the "splitting" tendency of Russian botany in that period.

William T. Stearn and Peter H. Davis produced *Peonies of Greece: A Taxonomic and Historical Survey of the Genus* Paeonia in Greece (1984), a handsome book, beautifully illustrated. Ronald Melville published "The Affinity of *Paeonia* and a Second Genus of Paeoniaceae" (1983), in which he explained the status of the genus in a wider context.

Stephen G. Haw and Lucien A. Lauener (1990) introduced a new wave of studies on the Suffruticosa group with "A Review of the Infraspecific Taxa of *Paeonia suffruticosa* Andrews." Further work on the woody peonies was undertaken by the Chinese botanists Hong Tao, Zhang J. X., et al. (1992) in which they described three new species and raised *P. rockii* to specific status. In the second part of this work, Hong and Osti (1994) described a new species similar to *P. rockii* and described *P. spontanea* as a species. Yan Pei and D. Hong (1995) described *P. qiui* as a new species. D. Hong revised the status of *P. decomposita* and divided it into two subspecies.

During a visit to China in 1997, I examined the type specimens for the Chinese species, particularly the newly described ones. The present work reflects my interpretations of these specimens; I believe that in some cases (though by no means all), the new species are no more than varieties or even forms of already established ones.

My own studies on *Paeonia* were published in *Acta Musei Richnoviensis* in 1997 and 1998. In these articles the genus is revised and classified, with many entities (particularly the Caucasian plants) combined and two new ones described. The systematic presentation and key in those articles and in the present book are based on the main morphological characters of root, flower structure, fruits, and seeds. Stearn's systematic description of the herbaceous species and his key are based more on leaves than on flowers and fruits, but in my treatment the leaf characters, while considered, are secondary. Another notable departure in my treatment is the reduction of all species of the section *Moutan* into a series of varietal ranks, so that *P. suffruticosa* is seen as a large complex uniformly characterized by vaginate staminodes.

CHAPTER 2

Morphology

This chapter introduces the structures found in the genus *Paeonia*, generally characterizing the parts of the plant that are important for identification. The figures display graphically some important classificatory features.

Roots

The roots are always fleshy. Figure 9 shows the seven main types of roots in the genus: (1) a vertical primary root with several to many secondary roots—the Suffruticosa type root found in all the woody peonies, typical of *Paeonia suffruticosa*; (2) more or less regular main roots with a headlike knob at the top and many secondary roots—the Lactiflora type, typical of *P. lactiflora*; (3) fasciculate main roots with many secondary roots, typical of *P. brownii*; (4) a tapering or oval root, typical of the *P. mascula* group; (5) fusiform or digitate form, in which cormlike, swollen roots grow directly from the rootstock or from loose attachments to it, then taper into thin roots, a type found in subsection *Paeonia*, typical of *P. officinalis*; (6) fusiform roots, characterized by a thick, irregular main root with swollen, cormlike roots on stringlike attachments, found in subsections *Anomalae* and *Obovatae*, typical of *P. anomala*; and (7) fusiform root, with a thin rootstock and many subglobular, swollen, short segments resembling a chain coral, found in *P. tenuifolia*. Generally, the shape and size of the roots are characteristic for each species.

Stem and Leaves

Figure 10 employs a schematic drawing of one species, *Paeonia tenuifolia*, to show the parts of a typical herbaceous peony. The basal sheaths at the base of the stem are in fact modified petioles.

The leaves may be ternate or pinnate, ranging from biternate to multiply divided. They provide very important morphological characters in the identification of species; for this reason, drawings of foliage accompany the species descriptions in this book. Leaf form is less variable among the woody species than among the herbaceous ones. Many herbaceous species have 2 types of leaves on the same plant: single leaves growing from the base (usually more developed),

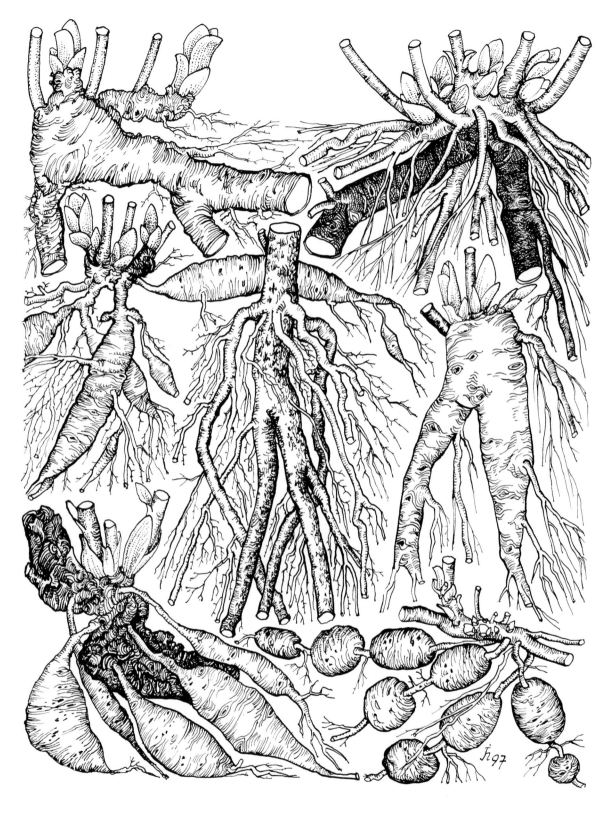

Figure 9. *Paeonia* roots. 1: *P. brownii.* 2: *P. lactiflora.* 3: *P. officinalis.*
4: *P. suffruticosa.* 5: *P. mascula.* 6: *P. anomala.* 7: *P. tenuifolia.*

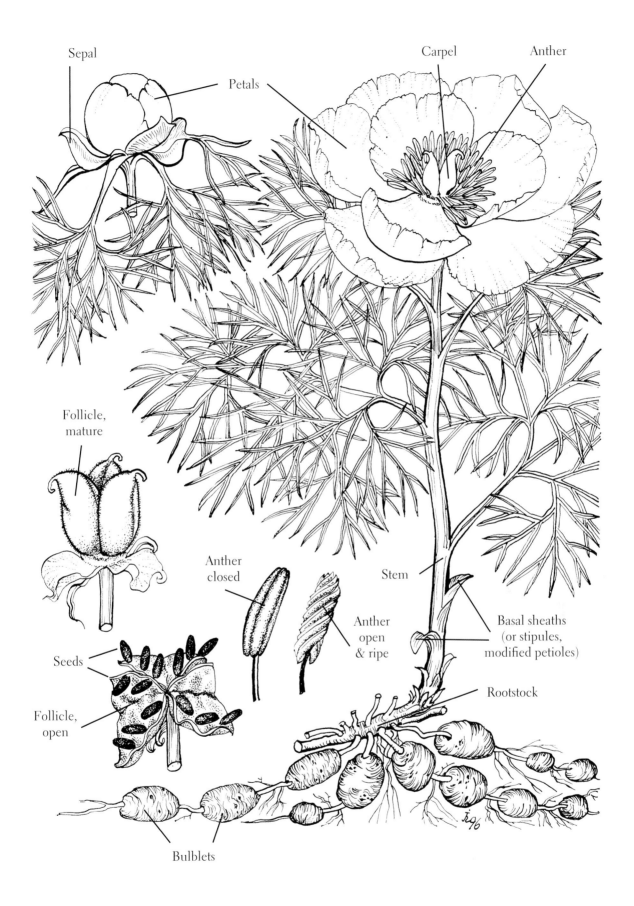

Sepal

Petals

Carpel

Anther

Follicle,
mature

Anther
closed

Anther
open
& ripe

Stem

Seeds

Follicle,
open

Basal sheaths
(or stipules,
modified petioles)

Rootstock

Bulblets

Figure 10. Schematic drawing of *Paeonia tenuifolia*.

and leaves on flowering stems that are alternate, long-stalked, and without stipules. The upper-most leaves on the flower stalk may be reduced to a single, entire leaflet.

The flowering stems vary in height from 10 cm (4 in.) in *Paeonia tenuifolia* "*lithophila* type*" to 3 m (10 ft.) or more in *P. lutea*. The height of an individual plant's flowering stem depends to some extent on its growing conditions.

Flowers

The flowers of most species are borne singly; several flowers per stem are borne by some woody species and the herbaceous species *Paeonia emodi*, *P. lactiflora*, and *P. veitchii*. The time of flowering in nature ranges from the end of February (*P. corsica*) to the end of June (*P. veitchii*). The parts of the flower are labeled in Figure 10.

The shape and number of sepals are characteristic for each species. In subgenus *Onaepia*, the sepals are rigid, almost covering the entire petal and they are quite distinct from the stem leaves. The fully open corolla is subglobose. The petals never spread to a fully horizontal position resulting in a cup-shaped flower, a feature also particularly noticeable in *P. potaninii* var. *trollioides* (subgenus *Moutan*) and *P. peregrina* (subgenus *Paeonia*). In subgenus *Albiflora*, there is a gradual transition in form from the outer to the inner sepals. Most of the species have flowers that open widely.

The petals vary in size and shape from species to species. Petals are nearly round and smooth-edged in *Paeonia obovata* and *P. potaninii* var. *trollioides*. Relatively narrow petals are found in *P. mairei*. Petals of *P. anomala* are distinctly edged with fine lace and the larger-flowered woody peonies have distinctly ruffled, fluted petals and many have distinct V-shaped notches along their edges.

Corolla size ranges from 3 cm (ca. 1 in.) in *Paeonia brownii* to more than 20 cm (8 in.) in *P. suffruticosa* subsp. *rockii*. This size too depends partly on growing conditions. The color range includes white and cream, many shades of pink and rose, light and dark reds, crimson, brownish purple, yellow, and coppery orange. Pink flowers often exhibit zones of darker and lighter pigment, creating a lovely bicolored effect. In some species, the pink flowers may fade as they age, or cream-colored flowers may develop a pink flush in time.

The disc is a fleshy outgrowth between the stamens and carpels. It is relatively inconspicuous in the Eurasian herbaceous species, such as *Paeonia officinalis*, but much more developed in the Chinese woody species and the North American *P. brownii*.

The carpels are free to the base. Their number varies from one in *Paeonia emodi* to as many as six in *P. delavayi* and up to eight in *P. veitchii*.

The stamens are numerous (usually about 140), with slender white, pink, or purple filaments; the anthers are usually yellow (rarely pink), dehiscing marginally, with very abundant yellow pollen. The pollen grains are spheroid prolate, tricolporate, with the furrows (colpi) narrow and extending almost to the poles, the exine finely reticulate, 25–40 micrometers long (Stearn and Davis 1984).

Seeds and Fruit

The follicles (seed pods) can be classified into four main types (Figure 11): (1) the Suffruticosa type—slim, erect, semi-open follicles, typical of *Paeonia suffruticosa*; (2) the Delavayi type—

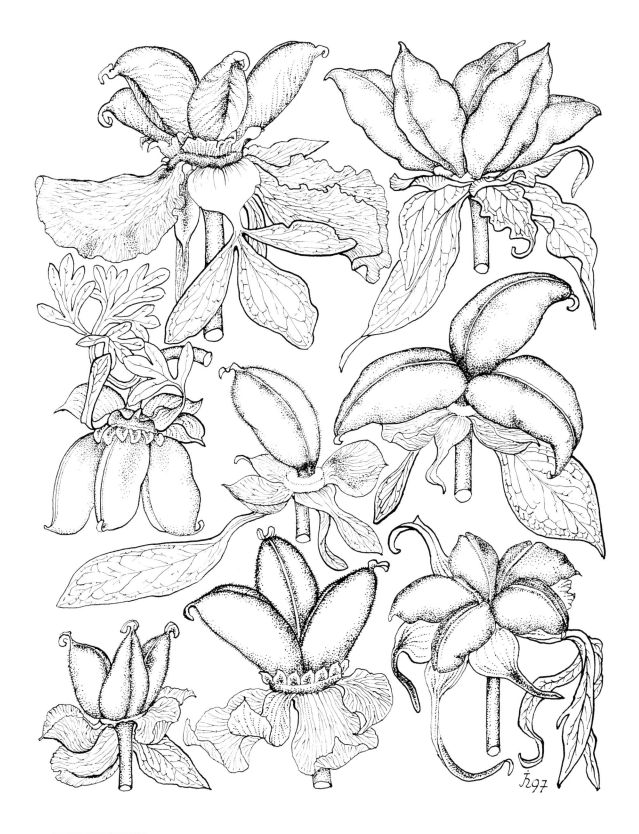

Figure 11. *Paeonia* mature follicles. 1: *P. suffruticosa*. 2: *P. delavayi*.
3: *P. brownii*. 4: *P. emodi*. 5: *P. officinalis*. 6: *P. lactiflora*. 7: *P. mlokosewitschii*.
8: *P. veitchii*.

1		2
3	4	5
6	7	7

erect, semi-open follicles with thick walls, typical of *P. delavayi*, *P. lutea*, and *P. potaninii*; (3) the Brownii type—pendent, half-open follicles with thin walls, found in *P. brownii*; and (4) the Mascula type—the erect follicles of most herbaceous species. Figure 12 (bottom row) displays three of kinds of peony follicles.

Peony seeds are brown to black, smooth, and relatively large. Their forms, displayed in Figure 12, can be grouped by size, shape, and color as follows: (1) cylindrical, ranging in size from those of *Paeonia tenuifolia* (4 × 8 mm) to the huge seeds of *P. lutea* (18 × 10 mm); (2) quadrangular-cylindrical, as in *P. suffruticosa* subsp. *rockii*; (3) regularly ovate, as in *P. emodi*; (4) irregularly ovate, as in *P. lactiflora*; and (5) almost globular, as in *P. mlokosewitschii*. The number of seeds in the follicle correlates with the size and shape of the seeds; that is, when the follicle contains a larger number of seeds, the seeds tend to be smaller and more irregular. For example, when a follicle of *P. suffruticosa* is very full, almost all the seeds are nearly regularly quadrangular, but when the follicle has only a few seeds, they are regularly cylindrical. The same is true of *P. anomala*, *P. brownii*, *P. delavayi*, *P. lactiflora*, *P. lutea*, *P. potaninii*, *P. veitchii*, and others. The inner part of the follicles in some species is coated with a brilliant red membrane, which is very ornamental when open and probably serves to attract birds that distribute the seeds.

Cytology

The basic chromosome number throughout the genus is 5 ($n = 5$). The size and morphology of the chromosomes differ little in the Old World species, but Stebbins and Ellerton (1939) stated that the American species are distinguished cytologically from the Old World species by the terminal localization of pachytene pairing and extensive reciprocal interchange of chromosome segments. Some peony species have 20 as their somatic chromosome number instead of 10, that is, some species are tetraploids ($2n = 20$), and some are diploids ($2n = 10$).

Saunders and Stebbins (1938) discussed the possibilities of hybridization between various species. They reported that diploid species do not cross easily with each other, but tetraploid species intercross naturally when growing near one another. The diploid species *Paeonia lactiflora* is difficult to cross with other diploid species but crosses easily with the tetraploid species. The chromosomal makeup of the resulting hybrids has not been well studied, but experience shows that they are not necessarily sterile. The diploid *P. mlokosewitschii* and the tetraploid *P. wittmanniana*, though taxonomically close to each other, are not very interfertile. Saunders and Stebbins carried out 54 pollinations but obtained only 8 F_1 plants. Stebbins noted complete interfertility between *P. delavayi* and *P. lutea* and between *P. veitchii* and *P. veitchii* var. *woodwardii*. The plants of each pair are without doubt closely related, but each member of the pair has sufficient morphological distinctiveness to be considered a separate taxon. No triploids have been reported in the wild, but triploid plants have been found among garden hybrids (Stern 1946). Descriptions of some F_1 and F_2 hybrids are detailed in Wister (1962). Stearn and Davis (1984) stated,

> Diploid as well as tetraploid populations were found in *Paeonia mascula* and *P. clusii*, whereas all populations of *P. peregrina* and *P. parnassica* were tetraploid. However, diploid plants of *P. peregrina* have been found in Yugoslavia which do not differ morphologically from the tetraploids.

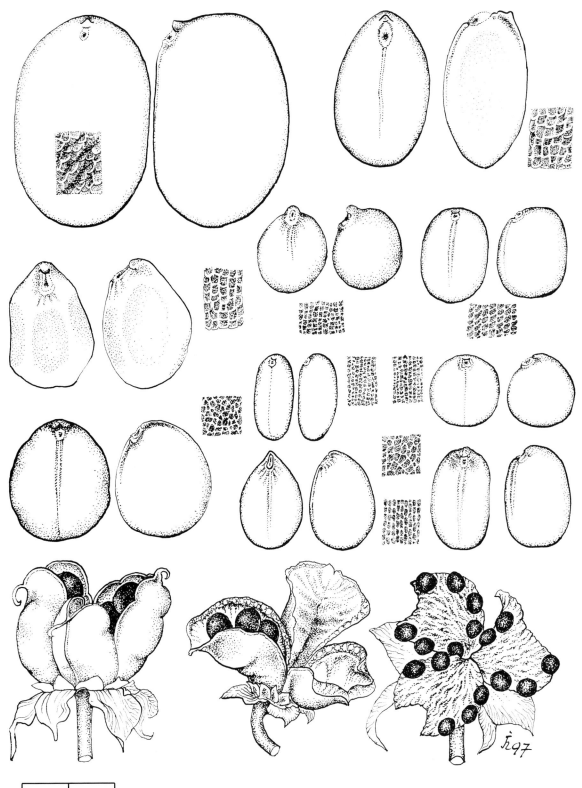

Figure 12. (top rows) *Paeonia* seeds, with detail of seed surface. 1: *P. lutea*.
2: *P. brownii*. 3: *P. lactiflora*. 4: *P. emodi*. 5: *P. mlokosewitschii*. 6: *P. obovata*.
7: *P. tenuifolia*. 8: *P. corsica*. 9: *P. anomala*. 10. *P. veitchii*. (bottom row)
Paeonia follicles. 11: *P. lutea*. 12: *P. brownii*. 13: *P. emodi* subsp. *sterniana*.

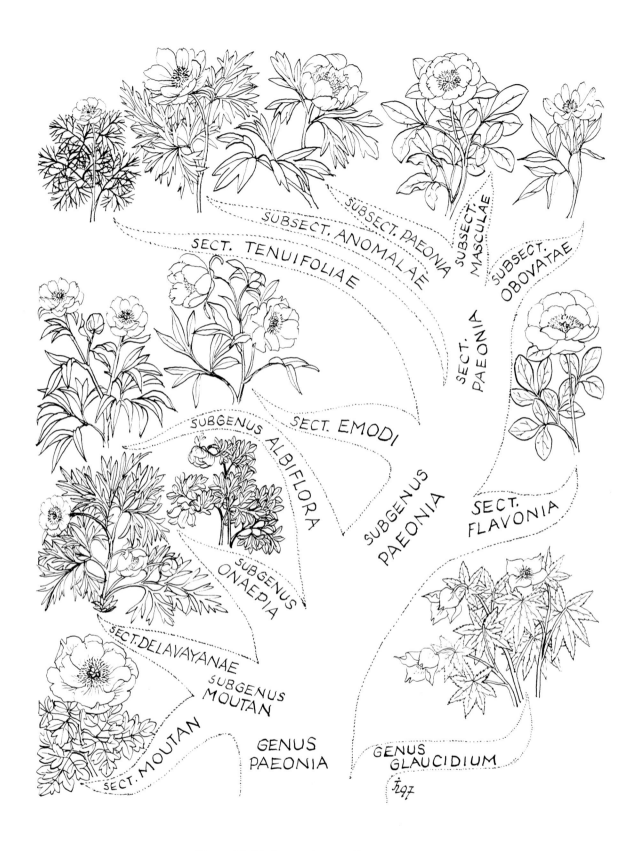

Figure 13. Phylogenetic tree of genus *Paeonia*.

CHAPTER 3

The Paeoniaceae and Its Affinities

The genus *Paeonia* was considered for a long time to belong in the family Ranunculaceae, until Rudolphi separated it in 1830, along with the monotypic genus *Glaucidium*, and established the family Paeoniaceae. Discussions of the wider affinities of *Paeonia* have centered on characteristics that distinguish it from the Ranunculaceae and two other families, the Magnoliaceae and the Dilleniaceae (a mostly tropical and woody family).

The first botanist to suggest that *Paeonia* be placed in its own family was Friedrich G. Bartling (1830). Wilson C. Worsdell (1908) supported this view based on a study of woody anatomy, a position accepted by Masao Kumazawa (1935). Edred J. H. Corner (1946) introduced an argument that became central to discussions of this topic, the centrifugal development of the fasciculate stamens in *Paeonia*, but he claimed that this indicated a relationship with the Dilleniaceae. A number of workers who followed (Melchior and Werdermann 1954, Eames 1961, Dickison 1967, Thorne 1968, Cronquist 1968) accepted Corner's suggestion, but Sawada (1971) rejected it based on differences in the floral vasculature of the two groups.

In the Magnoliaceae and Dilleniaceae, the floral vasculature is stemlike and consists of anthostrobili; in the Ranunculaceae and Paeoniaceae, there is no floral stele above the level of the sepals, and the reproductive organs are supplied by veins branching off from those of the sepals or tepals. The leaf venation of the Paeoniaceae is similar to patterns found within the Ranunculaceae, but quite distinct from that found in the Dilleniaceae. The differences in vasculature in both flowers and leaves between the Ranunculaceae and Paeoniaceae on one hand, and the Dilleniaceae and Magnoliaceae on the other, are very ancient in evolutionary terms.

Several other characters figured in this controversy. *Paeonia* has a nectariferous disc; nectaries of various kinds are found in the Ranunculaceae, but not in the Dilleniaceae. The Paeoniaceae and Dilleniaceae share the characters of tricolporate pollen and seeds with arils; however, Ronald Melville (1983) argued that these resemblances are more likely to result from parallel evolution than from anciently close relationship.

Paeonia and *Glaucidium* both have a basic chromosome number of $n = 5$, but this does not occur in either the Ranunculaceae or the Dilleniaceae. This combines with other characters to bolster the inclusion of *Glaucidium* in the Paeoniaceae. Michio Tamura (1972) used chromosome number as a reason for separating the Paeoniaceae, although he proposed a mono-generic family, Glaucidiaceae, for *Glaucidium*. Melville (1983) rejected this proposal.

Melville (1983) supported the establishment of the Paeoniaceae with its two genera, citing their shared chromosome numbers as well as "fasciculate stamens with centrifugal development, follicles with two grooves, dehiscing along both sutures, ovules with thick integuments, [and] vessels often with scalariform plates." On the same grounds, he excluded the genus *Hydrastis*, which some previous workers had suggested should be included in the Paeoniaceae.

Melville distinguished the Paeoniaceae from the Ranunculaceae in the arrangement of the vascular supply to the androecium (male reproductive organs). In the Ranunculaceae in general, the stamen traces are attached directly to erect longitudinal strands. In the Paeoniaceae, these longitudinal strands are absent, and the stamens are born on dichotomous trusses radiating laterally in the receptacle. Moreover, Melville noted that vessels with scalariform perforation plates are common in the Paeoniaceae, but absent in the Ranunculaceae.

It is unclear from Melville's argument whether the Paeoniaceae are considered an offshoot of the Ranunculaceae or a closely related branch descending from a common ancestor. The scalariform perforation plate mentioned earlier "is accepted as a primitive character in the Angiosperms," but conversely, "Study of leaf evolution in the Ranunculaceae has demonstrated that the palmate or palmatifid leaf represents an intermediate stage and that the ternato-pinnate leaf of *Paeonia* is more advanced."

Figure 13 is a phylogenetic tree which offers a graphic display of genus *Paeonia* (and *Glaucidium*), with its subgenera, sections, and subsections. In the ensuing chapters we will see that not only structural characteristics but also geographic distribution reinforce this view of the evolution of the genus.

CHAPTER 4

Distribution

Peonies are native only in the Northern Hemisphere in both the Old and New World. Species occur through much of Eurasia. The southernmost occurrences of herbaceous species are in northwest Africa (about 35°N) and the genus reaches its northern limits near the Arctic Circle on the Kola Peninsula of Russia (67°N). There are population centers in western Europe, the Balkans and Greece, Asia Minor and the Caucasus, the Himalayas, western China, Siberia, and Japan. The richest concentrations of subgenus *Paeonia* are in the Mediterranean region and the Caucasus. Woody peonies of subgenus *Moutan* are limited to the hill regions of western China, most of them in Yunnan and Sichuan provinces where they reach the southern limit of the entire genus (25°N). *Paeonia brownii*, the single species of subgenus *Onaepia*, inhabits the U.S. Pacific Coast and adjacent inland regions.

Climatic patterns differ greatly over this vast region. Most areas where peonies grow have temperate to cold climates with precipitation throughout the year. A significant center of the genus can be found around the shores of the Mediterranean, a warm region where precipitation occurs as rain from fall through early spring and where summers are hot and dry (as they are in the American localities of the genus), and in the eastern Himalayas, where winters are cool and dry and most moisture arrives with monsoon rains in late summer to fall. Obviously, certain sections of the genus have adapted to particular regions, but it is remarkable how well almost every species can be grown in gardens outside its homeland. The most striking adaptation to climate is seen in species from arid-summer regions, which make growth during winter and spring, then survive the summer as dormant tubers; yet even these species can be grown in areas of summer rainfall if given excellent drainage.

Most of the European species and populations are concentrated in southern Europe, where they grow in brushy *macchia* (similar to the vegetation known as chaparral in the United States) or open woodland. Some taxa of subsection *Masculae* can reach subalpine meadows or forests. Northern populations of *Paeonia anomala* in Scandinavia and northwestern Russia are typically found in open forest; however, these populations are not as dense as those in Siberia.

The Greek species are mostly plants of low and middle elevations where summers are hot and dry. Their typical habitats are open woodland and rocky slopes.

In Turkey, species of subsection *Masculae* grow mostly at low elevations in regions with very dry summers. By contrast, *Paeonia wittmanniana* grows in the eastern Pontus Mountains at higher elevations, where the weather is much moister in the summer.

The Caucasus is a patchwork of many vegetation types. *Paeonia tenuifolia* grows here at low elevations in meadows dotted with sparse shrubs, and *P. daurica* in dry open places, also at lower elevations. The yellow-flowered species—*P. mlokosewitschii* and *P. wittmanniana*—are found in much moister situations, inhabiting well-watered mountain forests and moist subalpine meadows; in cultivation they need much more water than the other species.

The hardy peonies of Siberia inhabit open woodland, steep slopes, and forest edges. These species, especially *Paeonia anomala*, sometimes form monocultures with hundreds of thousands of plants covering a large area. They always grow in good mountain soils with plenty of humus. *Paeonia veitchii* inhabits much moister woodland.

In China, members of section *Moutan* always grow in open forest or on rocky slopes at moderate altitudes. Species of section *Delavayanae* can grow much higher. For example, *Paeonia lutea* can reach 4000 m (13,000 ft.) in subalpine rhododendron-fir forest, where it luxuriates in the humus soil. The Delavayanae peonies, however, are also found at much lower elevations, in the dry lowlands or foothills.

Paeonia brownii of the western United States occurs in semidesert at higher elevations. It grows on open slopes and at the edges of woodland. The climate here is sometimes snowy in winter (though not very cold), and the summers are very hot and dry.

Conservation

These very ornamental plants are still dug from the wild. Populations have been devastated and many have disappeared. Restricting collection is not helpful, in my opinion, because enforcing bans on collecting plants is next to impossible in the regions where many peonies grow. The best solution is to propagate plants from wild-collected seeds and make them available to nurseries and gardeners, thus relieving the pressure on wild plants.

The problem is the same everywhere: the most dangerous animal for any part of nature is the human. Many peony species are narrowly endemic, with very limited numbers of individual plants, and their populations can be destroyed easily. For example, the Mediterranean *Paeonia clusii*, *P. rhodia*, and varieties of *P. mascula* subsp. *hellenica* among others, are endemic to small areas on small islands. These are very susceptible to human collection, livestock, and agriculture. Most are more easily available as seed-propagated plants that should be sought in preference to wild plants.

In the old Czech medicinal text *Herbarea* are notes on wild *Paeonia officinalis*. The species was not rare in the Czech Republic and the rest of central Europe in the 16th century; despite being dug for medicinal use, the wild populations still survived. Now they no longer exist. The reasons are probably that they were dug for ornamental use in private gardens, and their environment was transformed into cropland, buildings, or artificially cultivated forest.

CHAPTER 5

Synopsis of the Genus *Paeonia* and Its Close Relatives

The following synopsis incorporates revisions published in *Acta Musei Richnoviensis* (Halda 1997, 1998). The new infrageneric classification is divided into four subgenera and six sections. Beyond this classification, the present synopsis includes many new combinations, particularly among the Caucasian and Chinese taxa.

The key following should be accessible to the gardener as well to the botanist. For guidance with the technical terms, see the discussion and illustrations in chapter 2. In using the keys and the descriptions that follow, the reader should remember that white-flowered individuals occur in some normally red-flowered species; however, atypical white forms are not as common in *Paeonia* as in some other genera.

Family Paeoniaceae

Family Paeoniaceae Rudolphi, Syst. Orb. Veg. 61 (1830). Ranunculaceae Tribus V. Paeoniaceae de Candolle, Prodromus Systematis Naturalis Regni Vegetabilis 1: 64 (1824); Paeoniae (Bernhard 1833) Prantl (1888); Paeonioideae Hutchinson (1923).

Key to family Paeoniaceae
   Leaves ternately compound; sepals persistent; seeds subglobose or cylindrical, not winged; follicles (1–)3–5 . . . . ***Paeonia***
   Leaves palmate or pinnately divided; sepals caducus; seeds flat, winged; follicles 2 . . . . ***Glaucidium***

Genus *Glaucidium*

Glaucidium Siebold & Zuccarini, Abh. Akademie. Muench. iv. II. (1845) 184. Family Glaucidiaceae Tamura, Botanical Magazine, Tokyo, 85: 40 (March 1972). Family Ranunculaceae. *Glaucidium paradoxum* Makino in Botanical Magazine, Tokyo, 24: 71 (1910); *Glaucidium pinnatum* Finet & Gagnepain in Bulletin de la Société botanique de France 51: 392 (1905).

TYPE SPECIES: *Glaucidium palmatum* Siebold & Zuccarini.

DESCRIPTION: Herbaceous perennial; rhizome very short and stout; stem unbranched with one to three leaves; leaves alternate, petiolate, pinnately or palmately dissected and serrated. Flowers solitary, 3.5–8 cm (1.4–3 in.) across. Sepals petaloid, four, pale lilac-pink to white. Stamens 20–200, numerous. Carpels one or two with 15–20 ovules. Marginal placentation. Fruits nonfleshy with dehiscent carpels. Seeds winged and compressed. Seedling epigeal with two cotyledons.

DISTRIBUTION: Woodlands, thickets to subalpine, central Honshu and Hokkaido, Japan, and Sichuan Province, China. $2n = 20$.

Key to genus *Glaucidium*
   Leaves palmate with 7–12 lobes . . . . *Glaucidium palmatum*
   Leaves compound, pinnate . . . . *Glaucidium pinnatum*

Glaucidium palmatum

DESCRIPTION: As for the genus. Height 25–60 cm (10–24 in.). Leaves simple, palmate with up to 12 lobes, margin serrate, up to 20 cm (8 in.) across. Flowering May to July. Seeds to 1 cm (0.4 in.), flattened, winged.

DISTRIBUTION: Hokkaido, Japan, in woodlands.

COMMENT: This is a desirable woodland garden ornamental perennial. Requires a protected damp spot that does not experience drought conditions. Prefers humusy soils in damp shade. Suited to alpine house cultivation. Flowers have a silky texture that emphasizes the delicacy of flower colors. Usually propagated by seed, which takes three years or longer to bloom. A white-flowered form is especially striking, but is rarely available. See Figures 14, 15.

Glaucidium pinnatum Finet & Gagnepain in Bulletin de la Société botanique de France 51: 392 (1905).

DESCRIPTION: Differs from *G. palmatum* by the two pinnately compound leaves with four or six opposite leaflets and a single terminal leaflet. Leaflets 2–2.5 cm wide (0.75–1 in.), 5–8 cm (2–3 in.) long. Flowers solitary, 3.5 cm (1.4 in.) across. Sepals four, petaloid pink. Single carpel 1 cm (0.4 in.) long. Seed and fruit not known.

DISTRIBUTION: China, central Sichuan Province in the area of Kangding (Chen-keou-tin).

COMMENT: A less common species with distinct foliage. Flowers smaller than those of *G. palmatum*. Cultivation unknown but probably similar to *G. palmatum*. Not known to be in cultivation at this time. See Figure 14.

Genus *Paeonia*

Paeonia Linnaeus, Species Plantarum 1: 530 (1753). Lectotype: *P. officinalis* Linnaeus sensu stricto (var. *alfa feminea*).

DESCRIPTION: Small deciduous shrubs or perennial herbs dying down in the winter. Roots more or less succulent or tuberous. Leaves alternate, large, at least the lower ones simply biternate or further divided. Flowers solitary or several, 6–20 cm (2.4–8 in.) across. Sepals 3–8, imbricate, herbaceous, persistent. Petals 6–18, broad, red, pink, white, or yellow. Stamens numerous,

Figure 14. *Glaucidium* leaves: (top) G. *palmatum*, (bottom) G. *pinnatum*.

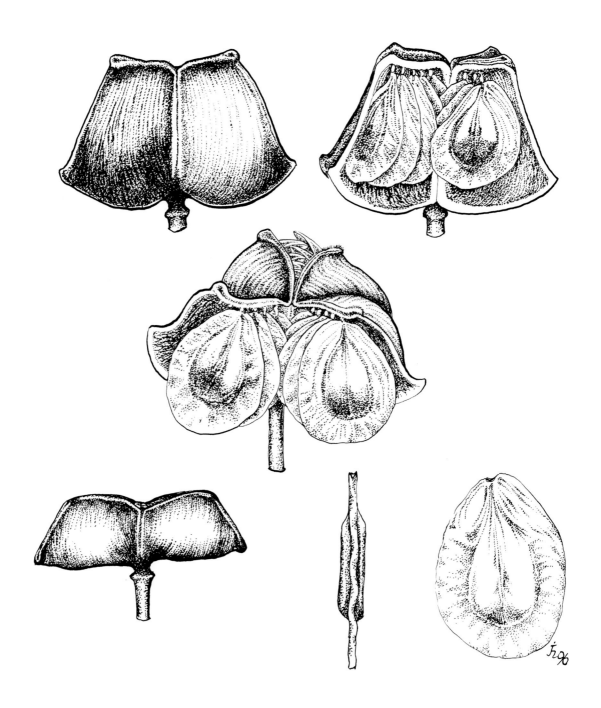

Figure 15. *Glaucidium palmatum* floral structure: (top row, left to right) mature follicles, ×2;
cross section of follicle, ×2; (middle row) split follicles when ripe, ×2.5;
(bottom row, left to right) immature follicles, ×2; seed side view; seed flat view, ×3.

Glaucidium palmatum, two color forms

Glaucidium pinnatum

maturing centrifugally. Carpels one to six, sometimes to eight, glabrous or pubescent, multi-ovulate, surrounded at base by a depressed fleshy disc. Styles with a circinate stigmatic area. Fruit a group of horizontally spreading follicles with numerous seeds in two rows; fertile seeds blackish or brown, borne on a more or less fleshy funicular aril; sterile seeds smaller, red and juicy.

Outline of Genus *Paeonia*

Over two hundred names have been published in the genus *Paeonia*. Most of these are duplicate names (synonyms) for a fairly small group of valid species. The present treatment validates only twenty-five species in four subgenera.

The American herbaceous peonies are recognized as a distinct subgenus and here considered as a single species with two subspecies. Their relationship to other subgenera suggests a closer tie to the woody species, but much remains to be determined here.

The large numbers of Old World herbaceous species are best known, but their systematics have been unclear. A few are so distinct that they have long warranted separation at various taxonomic levels: *Paeonia emodi, P. lactiflora, P. mlokosewitschii* (along with the obvious closely related *P. wittmanniana*), and *P. tenuifolia* are each given distinct and separate identities at the section or subgenus level.

The other herbaceous species (most in section *Paeonia*) have been confused for many years. There are good reasons. Some, such as *Paeonia anomala*, are very widespread and variable; others are found in numerous disjunct populations often on small islands such as *P. mascula* and various Mediterranean species. The current review places the majority of herbaceous peonies in four subsections that range across Western Europe to the Far East.

The woody species are in many ways more coherent, there are fewer of them, and they occupy a smaller area of distribution. Recent field and laboratory research has resurrected and originated a number of "new" species names. This book reduces the plethora of names to five species in two sections.

The taxonomic rearrangement that follows is based on decades of field research, herbarium study, and growing most species in cultivation. The outline summarizes the taxonomy and includes both familiar and strange names. Some names may reflect new associations.

Genus *Paeonia*
Subgenus *Paeonia*
  Section *Paeonia*
    Subsection *Paeonia*
      1. *P. officinalis*
        Subspecies *officinalis*
        Subspecies *banatica*
        Subspecies *humilis*
        Subspecies *villosa*
      2. *P. peregrina*
      3. *P. parnassica*
      4. *P. clusii*
      5. *P. rhodia*
    Subsection *Masculae*
      6. *P. mascula*
        Subspecies *mascula*
        Subspecies *arietina*
        Subspecies *russoi*
        Subspecies *atlantica*
        Subspecies *hellenica*
          Variety *hellenica*
          Variety *icarica*
        Subspecies *bodurii*
        Subspecies *kesrouanensis*
      7. *P. daurica*
        Subspecies *daurica*
        Subspecies *lagodechiana*
      8. *P. coriacea*
      9. *P. corsica*
      10. *P. broteroi*
    Subsection *Anomalae*
      11. *P. anomala*
        Subspecies *anomala*
        Subspecies *hybrida*
      12. *P. veitchii*
        Subspecies *veitchii*
          Variety *veitchii*
          Variety *woodwardii*
        Subspecies *altaica*
    Subsection *Obovatae*
      13. *P. obovata*
        Subspecies *obovata*
          Variety *obovata*
          Variety *willmottiae*
        Subspecies *japonica*
      14. *P. mairei*
  Section *Tenuifoliae*
      15. *P. tenuifolia*
        Subspecies *tenuifolia*
        Subspecies *biebersteiniana*

Section *Emodi*
   16. *P. emodi*
      Subspecies *emodi*
      Subspecies *sterniana*
Section *Flavonia*
   17. *P. mlokosewitschii*
   18. *P. wittmanniana*
      Subspecies *wittmanniana*
      Subspecies *macrophylla*

Subgenus *Albiflora*
   19. *P. lactiflora*

Subgenus *Onaepia*
   20. *P. brownii*
      Subspecies *brownii*
      Subspecies *californica*

Subgenus *Moutan*
  Section *Moutan*
   21. *P. suffruticosa*
      Subspecies *suffruticosa*
      Subspecies *spontanea*
        Variety *spontanea*
        Variety *jishanensis*
        Variety *qiui*
      Subspecies *ostii*
      Subspecies *rockii*
        Variety *rockii*
        Variety *linyanshanii*
        Variety *yananensis*
   22. *P. decomposita*
      Subspecies *decomposita*
      Subspecies *rotundiloba*
  Section *Delavayanae*
   23. *P. delavayi*
   24. *P. lutea*
   25. *P. potaninii*
      Variety *potaninii*
      Variety *trollioides*

Key to genus *Paeonia*

1a. Roots succulent, not woody; stems herbaceous, deciduous 2
1b. Roots woody; stems woody, persistent . . . . Subgenus *Moutan*
2a. Leaves thin or coriaceous, margin entire, smooth 3
2b. Leaves chartaceous, margin scabrous, cartilaginous with rows of irregular serrate teeth [Subgenus *Albiflora*] . . . . 19. *P. lactiflora*

3a. Staminodial disc reaches more than one-third of gynoecium; petals coriaceous, slightly larger than sepals [Subgenus *Onaepia*] . . . . 20. *P. brownii*
13b. Staminodial disc small or poorly developed; petals thin, much larger than sepals . . . . Subgenus *Paeonia*

Subgenus *Paeonia*

Subgenus *Paeonia*
Subgenus *Paeonia* prop. Baker, Gardeners' Chronicle, ser. 3 (21): 779 (1884).
Subgenus *Paeon* (de Candolle) Seringe, Flora des Jardins 3: 193 (1849).
Section *Paeon* de Candolle, Prodromus Systematis Naturalis Regni Vegetabilis 1: 65 (1824).
Section *Albiflora* Salm-Dyck, Hortus Dyckensis, 365, 366 (1834).
Section *Compactae* Salm-Dyck, Hortus Dyckensis, 365, 366 (1834).
Section *Corralinae* Salm-Dyck, Hortus Dyckensis, 365, 366 (1834).
Section *Laciniatae* Salm-Dyck, Hortus Dyckensis, 365, 366 (1834).
Section *Lobatae* Salm-Dyck, Hortus Dyckensis, 365, 366 (1834).
Section *Macrocarpae* Salm-Dyck, Hortus Dyckensis, 365, 366 (1834).
Section *Microcarpae* Salm-Dyck, Hortus Dyckensis, 365, 366 (1834).
Section *Paeonia* Reichenbach, Repert. Herb. s. Nom. Gen. Pl. 191 (1841).
Section *Eupaeonia* Baillon, Adansonia 4: 56 (1863).
Section *Tripaeonia* Baillon, Adansonia 4: 56 (1863).
Section *Palearcticae # Herbaceae* Huth in Botanische Jahrbücher 14: 265 (1891).
Series *Chinenses* Komarov, Flora of the USSR 7: 25 (1937).
Series *Corallinae* (Salm-Dyck) Komarov, Flora of the USSR 7: 28 (1937).
Series *Dentatae* Komarov, Flora of the USSR 7: 33 (1937).
Series *Fissae* Komarov, Flora of the USSR 7: 34 (1937).
Series *Obovatae* Komarov, Flora of the USSR 7: 26 (1937).
DESCRIPTION: Stems herbaceous, annual, dying down at end of each growing season. Petals thin, much

Paeonia officinalis subsp. *officinalis*

P. officinalis var. *eufeminea* Ascherson & Graebner, Synopsis der Mitteleuropaischen Flora 5 (2): 555 (1923).

DESCRIPTION: Stem sparsely villous, soon glabrous, up to 70 cm (28 in.) tall. Lower leaves biternate, but the leaflets deeply cut into numerous narrow elliptic or narrow oblong acute segments which are up to 12 × 3 cm (4.75 × 1.1 in.), green and glabrous above, paler and sparsely villous or sometimes glabrous below; petiolules and petiole villous to glabrous. Flowers 9–13 cm (3.5–5 in.) across. Petals obovate, wide-spreading, bright red. Stamens 15 mm long, filaments red, anthers yellow. Carpels two or three, densely tomentose. Follicles ca. 30 mm long. Flowering April to May. $2n = 20$.

DISTRIBUTION: Southern and south-central Europe, from France to Hungary and Albania, growing on shrubby hills and in open woodland at altitudes from 100 to 1800 m (330 to 5940 ft.).

COMMENT: *Paeonia officinalis* subsp. *officinalis* has been widespread in cultivation for at least five hundred years. It grows well in the open garden and flowers freely. We collected this taxon many times, from the sea coast in Istria (Pula JJH690784) to Albania (Vlora JJH840633), as well as in the Italian Alps (Lago di Como JJH850742, Tessin JJH850793). Horticultural clones exist, including at least one double red and a very rare albino. Variations in floral size and color can be seen in the wild, but they are very uncommon (Boyd 1928). See Figure 16.

P. officinalis subsp. *banatica* (Rochel) Soo, Novenyfoldrajz 146 (1945).

P. banatica Rochel, Plantae Banatus Rariores 48: 11 (1828).

P. rosea Host, Flora Austriaca (Vienna) 2: 64 (1831), pro parte.

P. peregrina var. *banatica* (Rochel) Kittel, Taschenbuch der Flora Deutschlands, ed. 2, p. 790 (1844).

P. officinalis Linnaeus, sec. Kitaibel Add. Fl. Hung., ed. Kanitz, p. 184 (1864), non Linnaeus.

P. peregrina Miller, sec. Heuffel, Verhandlungen der kayserlich-königlichen zoologisch-botanischen Gesellschaft in Wien, p. 49 (1858).

P. feminea var. *banatica* (Rochel) Gurke in Richter, Plantae Europeae 2: 403 (1903).

P. officinalis var. *banatica* (Rochel) Ascherson & Graebner, Synopsis der Mitteleuropaischen Flora 5 (2): 556 (1923).

P. officinalis subvar. *banatica* (Rochel) Hayek, Prodro-

mus Florae Peninsulae Balcanicae 1: 298 (1924).

EPITHET: *banatica*, "from Banat," a region at the intersection of the borders of Hungary, Yugoslavia, and Romania.

DESCRIPTION: Differs from subsp. *officinalis* in having only the central leaflet deeply divided. Flowering April to May. $2n = 20$.

DISTRIBUTION: Hungary, Yugoslavia, and Romania, growing on open hills and shrubby slopes.

COMMENT: This taxon seems to be rare in cultivation, but it is a good candidate for the garden. Our collections from Romanian Banat (for example, Baie Herculane JJH660579) are vigorous plants from 50 to 60 cm (20 to 24 in.) tall, with large, light red flowers.

P. officinalis subsp. *humilis* (Retzius) Cullen & Heywood, Feddes Repertorium 69: 34 (1964).

P. humilis Retzius, Observationes botanicae 3: 35 (1783).

P. officinalis Linnaeus, sec. Gouan, Flora Monspeliaca 266 (1765).

P. villosa Desfontaines, Tableau de l'Ecole de Botanique du Museum d'Histoire Naturelle, Paris, 126 (1804).

P. paradoxa var. *leiocarpa* de Candolle, Prodromus Systematis Naturalis Regni Vegetabilis 1: 66 (1824).

P. peregrina var. *beta* de Candolle, Flore de France 5 (6): 643 (1815).

P. peregrina beta *leiocarpa* (de Candolle) Cosson, Notes Pl. Nouv. Rares Crit. 3: 93 (1851).

P. microcarpa Boissier & Reuter, Pugillus Plantarum Novarum Africae Borealis Hispaniaeque Australis 3 (1852).

P. peregrina var. *humilis* (Retzius) Huth in Botanische Jahrbücher 14: 270 (1891).

P. peregrina f. *leiocarpa* (de Candolle) Rouy & Foucaud, Flore de France 1: 145 (1893).

P. peregrina f. *microcarpa* (Boissier & Reuter) Rouy & Foucaud, Flore de France 1: 146 (1893).

P. feminea var. *humilis* (Retzius) Gurke in Richter, Plantae Europeae 2: 402 (1903).

P. leiocarpa Jordan in Jordan and Fourreau, Icones ad Floram Europeae 2: 38, t. 320 (1903).

P. modesta Jordan in Jordan and Fourreau, Icones ad Floram Europae 2: 38, t. 321 (1903).

P. feminea var. *humilis* (Retzius) Sampaio, Prodromus Florae Portug., p. 8 (1909–1911).

P. officinalis var. *humilis* (Retzius) Ascherson & Graebner, Synopsis der Mitteleuropaischen Flora 5 (2): 556 (1923).

Figure 16. *Paeonia officinalis* leaves: (top) subsp. *officinalis*, (bottom) subsp. *humilis*.

EPITHET: *humilis,* "low."

DESCRIPTION: Differs from subsp. *officinalis* in having leaflets cut into segments that are at most one-third of the total leaflet length; follicles glabrous; stems and petioles pubescent. Flowering April to May. $2n = 20$.

DISTRIBUTION: Southwestern Europe, growing in open woods, on shrubby slopes, and among rocks at altitudes from 200 to 1800 m (660 to 5940 ft.).

COMMENT: This taxon has probably been in cultivation for many years. It is a vigorous and long-lived plant, given suitable conditions. Out of our many collections, the most attractive is a dwarf form only 20 cm (8 in.) tall, with rose-red petals, from the eastern Pyrenees (Perpignan JJH900948); this should be propagated under a cultivar name, such as 'Perpignan'. See Figure 16.

P. officinalis subsp. villosa (Huth) Cullen & Heywood, Feddes Repertorium 69: 34 (1964).

P. peregrina var. *villosa* Huth in Botanische Jahrbücher 14: 270 (1891).

P. hirsuta Jaume St. Hilaire, Plantes de France 4: 1 (1809), non Miller (1768).

P. rosea Jaume St. Hilaire, Plantes de France 4: 2 (1809).

P. peregrina Miller, sec. Sims in Botanical Magazine, Tokyo, t. 1050 (1807).

P. officinalis Linnaeus, sec. Tenore, Flora Napolitana 1: 300 (1815), non Linnaeus, emend. Willdenow.

P. peregrina var. *beta* de Candolle, Flora France 5 (6): 643 (1815), pro parte.

P. paradoxa var. *fimbriata* Sabine in Transactions of the Horticultural Society, London 2: 276 (1817).

P. paradoxa Anderson in Transactions of the Linnean Society, London, 12: 280 (1818).

P. mollis Anderson in Transactions of the Linnean Society, London, 12: 282 (1818).

P. pubens Sims in Botanical Magazine, Tokyo, t. 2264 (1821).

P. russi Bivona, sec. Sweet, British Flower Garden 2: 122 (1825).

P. sessiliflora Sims in Botanical Magazine, Tokyo, t. 2648 (1826).

P. villosa Desfontaines, sec. Sweet, British Flower Garden, t. 113 (1826).

P. microcarpa Salm-Dyck, Hortus Dyckensis, 368 (1834).

P. lobata Desfontaines ex Reichenbach, Flora Germanica Excursoria 4: 123 (1839).

P. peregrina f. *paradoxa* (Anderson) Rouy & Foucaud, Flore de France 1: 145 (1893).

P. peregrina var. *paradoxa* (Anderson) Gautier, Cat. Rais. Flora Pyr.-Or. 71 (1898).

P. officinalis subsp. *euofficinalis* var. *paradoxa* (Anderson) Fiori & Paoletti, Flora Analitica d'Italia 1: 527 (1898).

P. feminea var. *villosa* (Desfontaines) Gurke in Richter, Plantae Europeae 2: 402 (1903).

P. peregrina var. *genuina* Lazara e Ibiza, Comp. Flora Espan. 2: 357 (1907).

P. officinalis var. *villosa* Ascherson & Graebner, Synopsis der Mitteleuropaischen Flora 5 (2): 555 (1923).

P. humilis var. *villosa* (Huth) F. C. Stern in Journal of the Royal Horticultural Society 68: 129 (1943).

P. humilis var. *villosa* f. *fimbriata* (Sabine) F. C. Stern, A Study of the Genus *Paeonia*, p. 107 (1946).

P. officinalis subsp. *huthii* A. Soldano in Atti della Societa Italiana di Scienze Naturali e del Museo Civico di Storia Naturale di Milano 133 (10): 114 (1992).

EPITHET: *villosa,* "villous, hairy."

DESCRIPTION: Differs from subsp. *officinalis* in having leaflets cut into segments that are at most one-third of the total leaflet length; follicles pubescent; stems and petioles floccose. Flowering April to May. $2n = 20$.

DISTRIBUTION: Southern France to central Italy, growing in dry macchia. Subspecies *villosa* grows in the same district of Montpellier as subsp. *humilis*, from which it differs only in its tomentose carpels.

COMMENT: Common in cultivation, where it may still be found under such old synonyms as *Paeonia paradoxa, P. microcarpa, P. lobata, P. rosea,* or *P. mollis;* the last is especially frequently encountered in lists. This subspecies grows and flowers well in the garden. Our several collections from southern France (Lozère JJH6607315, Cevennes JJH700733, Annot JJH840812) are uniform.

2. P. peregrina Miller, Gardeners Dictionary, ed. 8, no. 3 (1768).

P. byzantina Clusius, Rariorum Plantarum Historia, 279 (1601).

P. lobata Desfontaines, Tableau de l'Ecole de Botanique du Museum d'Histoire Naturelle, Paris, 126 (1804), nom. nud.

P. decora Anderson, Transactions of the Linnean Society, London 12: 273 (1818).

P. officinalis beta *lobata* (Desfontaines ex de Candolle) Lindley in Botanical Register, t. 819 (1824).

P. multifida Salm-Dyck, Hortus Dyckensis, 369 (1834).

P. officinalis Linnaeus, sec. Baumgarten, Enumeratio Stirpium Magno Transsilvaniae 2: 91 (1816).

P. romanica Brandza, Prodromul Florei Romane, p. 38 (1879–1883).

EPITHET: *peregrina*, "exotic, foreign."

DESCRIPTION: Stem glabrous, up to 90 cm (3 ft.) tall. Lower leaves biternate, but with some of the leaflets divided to the base so that there are in all 15–17 principal divisions; some of the divisions are deeply cut into two or three segments and the divisions lobed and coarsely toothed at the apex; leaflets 5–12 cm (2–4.75 in.) long, green and shining above, glaucous and slightly villous to glabrous below. Flowers 7–11 cm (2.75–4.4 in.) across. Petals strongly concave, obovate, rounded, 4.5–9 × 4 cm (1.75–3.5 × 1.5 in.), red. Stamens 20–25 mm long, filaments red, anthers yellow. Carpels two or three, densely tomentose. Follicles 20–30 × 10–20 mm. $2n = 20$.

DISTRIBUTION: Italy, the Balkan peninsula, southern Romania, and central Turkey, growing in ravines and open woodland at altitudes from 100 to 1500 m (330 to 4950 ft.).

COMMENT: We collected this species many times. Probably the most attractive form, pictured in the color plate, is from Dobruja, Romania (JJH670423). It has exceptionally large, rounded petals. A deservedly popular and first-rate garden plant, *Paeonia peregrina* has been in cultivation since the 15th century. It grows and flowers well in any well-drained position. Horticultural clones include 'Fire King' and 'Sunbeam'.

The name *Paeonia peregrina* is often misapplied in horticulture to forms of *P. officinalis*. The former species is readily distinguished at a glance, however, because its flowers never open widely. In the Peregrina group, only *P. parnassica* shares this feature; all the other species have widely open flowers. See Figures 17, 18.

3. *P. parnassica* Tzanoudakis, A Cytotaxonomic Study of the Genus *Paeonia* in Greece, p. 43 (1977).

P. peregrina var. *latifolia* Boissier, Flora Orientalis 1: 97 (1867).

EPITHET: *parnassica*, "from Mount Parnassus."

DESCRIPTION: Stem to 70 cm (28 in.), hirsute. Lower leaves biternate; lateral divisions with the terminal leaflet entire or deeply two- or three-lobed; leaflets and their lobes 9–13 in all, obovate to narrowly elliptic or lanceolate, acute or shortly acuminate, cuneate to attenuate at base; leaflets green above (pur-

plish when young), grayish green and densely pilose beneath; terminal petiolules of terminal leaflets 5–15 cm (2–6 in.). Flowers 8–12 cm (3–4.75 in.) across. Petals 9–12, obovate to obovate-orbicular, dark red. Filaments purplish. Carpels two or three, tomentose. Style circinate and stigmatic almost from base, ca. 1.5 mm broad. Flowering April to May. $2n = 20$.

DISTRIBUTION: Central and southern Greece in the regions of Karkaria, Parnassus, and Viotia, growing in open *Abies cephalonica* forest, open meadows, and among rocks at altitudes of 650 to 1500 m (2130 to 4950 ft.).

COMMENT: Our collections from different parts of Mount Parnassus (JJH870515, JJH89090032, and JJH940607) are uniform in size and color of flowers. This species can be distinguished from *Paeonia peregrina* by the shape of its silvery leaves and its dark violet flowers. Cultivation is as for *P. peregrina*, but this species prefers warmer, more protected sites and needs very good drainage. See Figure 17.

4. *P. clusii* F. C. Stern & Stearn in Curtis's Botanical Magazine 162: 9594 (1940).

P. cretica Clusius, Rariorum Plantarum Historia 1: 281 (1601).

P. cretica Tausch in Flora 9: 88 (1828), non Sabine (1824).

P. peregrina var. *glabra* Boissier, Flora Orientalis 1: 97 (1867).

P. peregrina var. *cretica* Huth in Botanische Jahrbücher 14: 270 (1891).

P. feminea var. *cretica* (Tausch) Gurke in Richter, Plantae Europeae 2: 403 (1903).

P. officinalis Linnaeus, sec. Sibthorp & Smith, Prodromus Flora Graec. 1: 369 (1806).

P. officinalis var. *cretica* (Tausch) Ascherson & Graebner, Synopsis der Mitteleuropaischen Flora 5 (2): 556 (1923).

P. officinalis var. *glabra* (Boissier) Hayek, Prodromus Florae Peninsulae Balcanicae 1: 298 (1924).

P. clusii subsp. *clusii* Tzanoudakis, A Cytotaxonomic Study of the Genus *Paeonia* in Greece, p. 23 (1977).

EPITHET: *clusii*, for the early botanist Clusius, who first described this species.

DESCRIPTION: Stems glabrous, pink or purplish, to 40 cm (16 in.) tall. Lower leaves biternate, but with leaflets dissected into 30 or more segments, some of which are themselves lobed or toothed; segments narrowly oblong to elliptic, tapering to the acute-acumi-

Paeonia officinalis subsp. *villosa*

Figure 17. Leaves of *Paeonia peregrina* (top) and *P. parnassica* (bottom).

Figure 18. *Paeonia peregrina*, engraving in *Hortus Eystettensis* (Besler 1613), as *P. bizanthina minor* (left) and *P. bizanthina major* (right).

Paeonia peregrina

Paeonia parnassica

nate apex, up to 6 × 1.8 cm (2.4 × 0.7 in.); green above, glaucous beneath, usually quite glabrous below. Flowers clover-scented, 7–10 cm (2.75–4 in.) across. Petals six–eight, obovate to broadly obovate, rounded, white, rarely flushed with pink. Stamens ca. 20 mm long, filaments pink, anthers golden-yellow. Carpels 2–4, densely white-tomentose, about 2 cm (0.75 in.) long at anthesis, style and stigma crimson. Follicles ca. 30 mm long. Flowering April to May. 2*n* = 20.

DISTRIBUTION: Greece, Crete, and Karpathos, growing on open hills, in Aleppo pine (*Pinus halepensis*) forest, on dry calcareous river beds, among rocks, and on shrubby slopes at altitudes from 200 to 2000 m (660 to 6600 ft.).

COMMENT: Clusius was the first botanist to mention the white peony of Crete. Bohemian botanist Franz Wilhelm Sieber (1789–1844), who visited Crete and gathered specimens in Lefka Ori, the White Mountains, made the first serious collection of it. Czech botanist Ignaz Friedrich Tausch (1793–1848) described these in 1828 as *Paeonia cretica*, but this name had been used earlier (in 1824) by Sabine, and Tausch's name is therefore invalid. *Paeonia clusii* is a most delightful Greek peony. Our plants from Lefka Ori (JJH840720) are vigorous and hardy. In proper conditions, this species can be grown in climates such as those of northern Germany or New York State if it is protected from summer rain and given a light cover in winter. See Figure 19.

5. *P. rhodia* Stearn in Gardeners' Chronicle, ser. 3 (110): 159, fig. 77 (1941).

P. clusii subsp. *rhodia* (Stearn) Tzanoudakis, A Cytotaxonomic Study of the Genus *Paeonia* in Greece, p. 25 (1977).

EPITHET: *rhodia*, "from Rhodes," an island in the Aegean Sea.

DESCRIPTION: Stem glabrous, reddish, to 40 cm (16 in.) tall. Lower leaves biternate, with all or nearly all leaflets divided; terminal leaflet of each set of three trifurcate, lateral leaflets usually bifurcate, sometimes entire and sometimes divided into three or four; leaflets entire, narrowly oblong-elliptic, apex acute or acuminate, base cuneate and sometimes confluent to the stem, thin and papery, up to 12 × 4 cm (4.75 × 1.5 in.), green above, pale green beneath, quite glabrous, shortly petiolulate, sometimes almost sessile. Flower white, about 7 cm (2.75 in.) across. Petals obovate to broadly obovate. Stamens ca. 15 mm long, filaments

red, anthers yellow. Carpels two to five, pubescent, with hairs white or flushed with red. Follicles up to 25 mm long. 2*n* = 10.

DISTRIBUTION: Greece, on the island of Rhodes, where it is endemic to Mount Profitis Elias, growing in coniferous forest of *Cupressus sempervirens* var. *horizontalis*, on open hills among limestone rocks, at altitudes of 300 to 700 m (990 to 2310 ft.).

COMMENT: *Paeonia rhodia* is closely allied to *P. clusii* but well distinguished by its foliage; the former has fewer leaflets and segments. This species was first collected in bloom in 1938, when Elsa Landby sent a specimen to the Royal Botanic Gardens, Kew. Our collections (JJH840799, JJH870512) are typical plants, but the former is much larger, almost 50 cm (20 in.) tall. A dry, well-drained site in a moderate climate suits this plant. See Figure 19.

Subsection *Masculae*

Subsection *Masculae* (F. C. Stern ex Uspenskaja) J. J. Halda stat. nov.

Paeonia section *Palearcticae* series *Masculae* F. C. Stern ex Uspenskaja in Byulleten Moskovskogo Obschchestva Ispytatelei Prirody, Biology, 92 (3): 83 (1987).

Paeonia section *Palearcticae Herbaceae* Huth in Botanische Jahrbücher 14: 256 (1891), pro parte.

Paeonia section *Paeonia* de Candolle, Prodromus Systematis Naturalis Regni Vegetabilis 1: 56 (1824), pro parte.

Paeonia section *Flavonia* Kemularia-Nathadze, Not. Syst. Geog. Inst. Bot. Tbiliss, Trudy Tbilisi Botanical Institute 21: 14 (1961), nom. nud.

Paeonia section *Paeon* Kemularia-Nathadze, Not. Syst. Geog. Inst. Bot. Tbiliss, Trudy Tbilisi Botanical Institute 21: 14 (1961).

Paeonia subsection *Foliolatae* Stern, A Study of the Genus *Paeonia*, p. 1 (1946).

DESCRIPTION: Leaves biternatisect; leaf segments entire, rarely bilaciniate or trilaciniate; petioles cylindrical with continuous ring of sclerenchyma.

TYPE SPECIES: *P. mascula* Miller.

6. *P. mascula* (Linnaeus) Miller, Gardeners Dictionary, ed. 8, art. *Paeonia*, no. 1 (1768).

P. officinalis var. *mascula* Linnaeus, Species Plantarum 1 (1753).

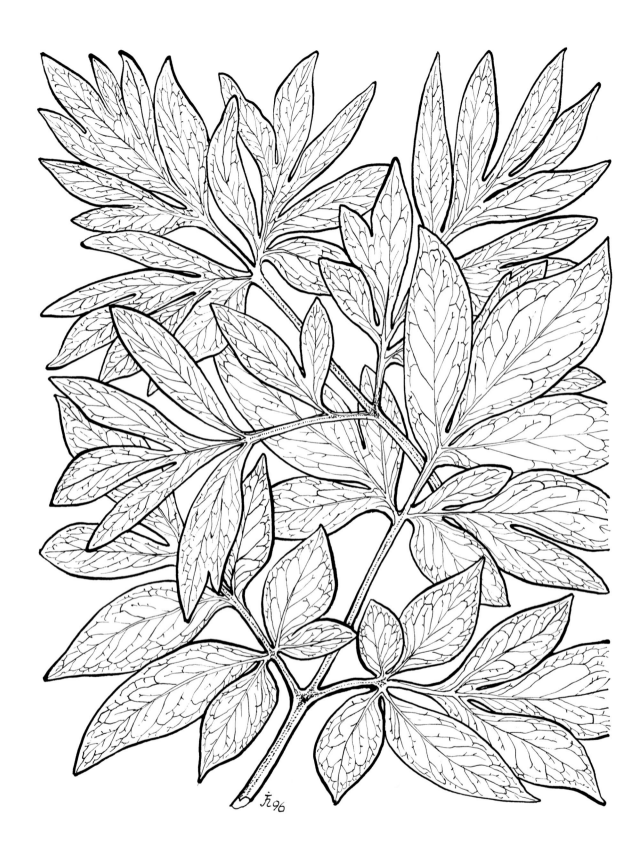

Figure 19. Leaves of (top) *Paeonia clusii* and (bottom) *P. rhodia*.

Paeonia clusii

Paeonia rhodia

EPITHET: *mascula*, "male."

Key to the subspecies of *P. mascula*
1a. Flowers pink, rose, or other shades of red . . . 2
1b. Flowers essentially white, may show colored veins 6
2a. Leaves glaucous, glabrous or sparsely hairy . . 3
2b. Leaves pubescent beneath 5
3a. Leaves glaucous beneath . . . . Subsp. *mascula*
3b. Leaves glabrous beneath 4
4a Carpels hairy; stigma a simple extension . . . . Subsp. *arietina*
4b. Carpels nearly hairless; a long stigma coiled at the end . . . . Subsp. *kesrouanensis*
5a. Lower leaves sparsely hairy . . . . . Subsp. *russoi*
5b. Lower leaves and petioles pubescent . . . . Subsp. *atlantica*
6a. Lower leaves biternate . . . . . . Subsp. *hellenica*
6b. Lower leaves ternate . . . . Subsp. *bodurii*

P. mascula subsp. *mascula*

P. mas Garsault, Pl. Anim. Med., t. 435 (1764).
P. corallina Retzius, Observationes botanicae 3: 34 (1783).
P. integra Murray in Commentationes Societatis Regiae Scientiarum Gottingensis 7: 92 (1786).
P. corallina var. *flavescens* (Presl) Gussone, Florae Siculae Synopsis 2 (1): 26 (1843).
P. corallina var. *corallina* (Retzius) Cosson, Compendium Florae Atlanticae 2: 52 (1886).
P. corallina var. *typica* Huth in Botanische Jahrbücher 14: 267 (1891).
P. corallina f. *corallina* (Retzius) Rouy & Foucaud, Flore de France 1: 144 (1893).
P. officinalis subsp. *corallina* var. *mascula* (Linnaeus) Fiori & Paoletti, Flora Analitica d'Italia 1: 527 (1898).
P. mascula var. *flavescens* (Presl) Gurke in Richter, Plantae Europeae 2: 400 (1903).
P. kavachensis Aznavour in Magyar Botanikai Lapok 16: 7 (1917).
DESCRIPTION: Roots tapering, somewhat carrotlike. Stem glabrous, up to 90 cm (3 ft.) tall. Lower leaves biternate, but sometimes with one or more leaflets bifurcate or trifurcate; leaflets 9–10(–12), broad elliptic, acute, cuneate at the base, dark green above, glaucous below, glabrous (or rarely with a few weak hairs on the back). Flowers 9–14 cm (3.5–5.5 in.) across. Petals obovate, red-rose. Stamens 15–20 mm long, filaments red, anthers yellow. Carpels three to five,

densely pubescent. Follicles 25–40 mm long. Flowering March to May. $2n = 20$.

DISTRIBUTION: Southern Europe, extending north to north-central France and Austria, and in Greece, Turkey, Lebanon, western Russia, Azerbaijan, Iraq, and Iran, growing on open hills, shrubby slopes, and dry meadows.

COMMENT: Subspecies *mascula* has been widespread in cultivation for at least five hundred years. It is vigorous and long-lived in suitable conditions. Gardeners particularly appreciate the unusually vivid rose hue of the flowers, which glows across the spring garden. It is easily raised from seed, often flowering within four years of sowing. From our numerous collections, the most ornamental forms are one from Armenia (Sevan JJH7206440) with purplish stems and dark purple petals, and another from eastern Turkey (Van JJH8710062, upper specimen) with dark fuchsia petals and green leaves. See Figures 20, 24.

P. mascula subsp. *arietina* (G. Anderson) Cullen & Heywood, Feddes Repertorium 69: 35 (1964).

P. arietina G. Anderson, Transactions of the Linnean Society, London, 12: 275 (1818).
P. arietina var. *andersoni* Lynch in Journal of the Royal Horticultural Society 12: 440 (1890).
P. arietina var. *cretica* (Sabine) Lynch in Journal of the Royal Horticultural Society 12: 440 (1890).
P. corallina var. *pubescens* Hayek, Prodromus Florae Peninsulae Balcanicae 1: 297 (1924).
P. cretica Sabine in Botanical Register, t. 819 (1824).
P. peregrina Miller, sec. Boissier, Flora Orientalis 1: 97 (1867), non Miller.
P. peregrina var. *latifolia* Boissier, Flora Orientalis 1: 97 (1867).
P. pubescens Schlosser & Vukotinovic, Flora Croatica 189 (1869).
P. rosea Host, Flora Austriaca (Vienna) 2: 64 (1831), pro parte, non Jaume St. Hilaire (1809).
P. russi Bivona, sec. Halacsy, Conspectus Florae Graecae 1: 35 (1901), non Bivona.
EPITHET: *arietina*, "horned," referring to the shape of the follicles.
DESCRIPTION: Differs from subsp. *mascula* in having leaves glabrous beneath, lower leaves with 12–16 narrowly elliptical leaflets. Flowering April to May. $2n = 20$.
DISTRIBUTION: Eastern Europe to eastern Turkey, growing on open hills and shrubby slopes at altitudes from 300 to 1400 m (990 to 4620 ft.).

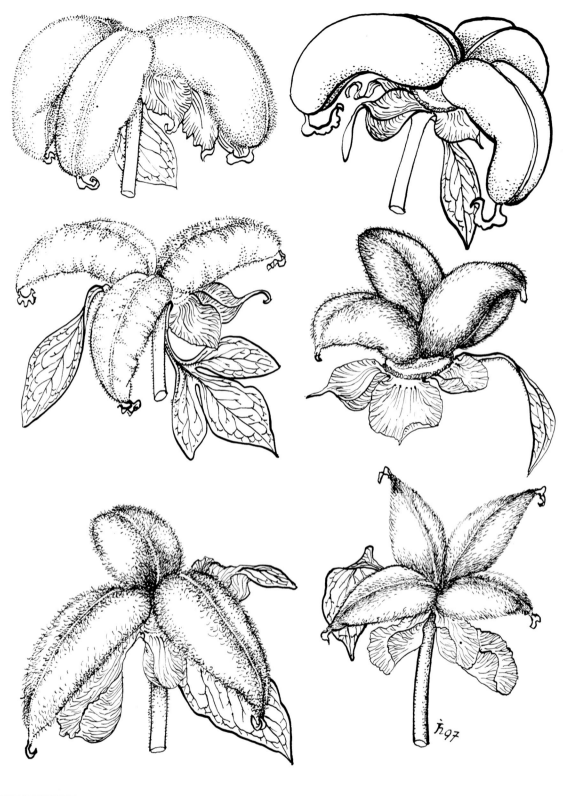

1	4
2	5
3	6

Figure 20. *Paeonia mascula* mature follicles. 1: subsp. *mascula*. 2: subsp. *russoi*.
3: subsp. *hellenica*. 4: subsp. *kesrouanensis*. 5: subsp. *arietina*. 6: subsp. *bodurii*.

Paeonia mascula subsp. *mascula*

Paeonia mascula subsp. *arietina*

COMMENT: We often collected this charming plant in eastern Turkey (for example, Erzurum JJH8709035). It is a common plant in cultivation (though garden plants under this name often prove to be hybrids), easily grown and flowering well while still young. See Figures 20, 21.

P. mascula subsp. *russoi* (Bivona) Cullen & Heywood, Feddes Repertorium 69: 35 (1964).

P. russi Bivona, Stirpium rariorum minisque cognitarum in Sicilia 4: 12 (1816).

P. corallina var. *pubescens* Moris, Flora Sardoa 1: 64, t. 4 (1837).

P. corallina var. *russi* (Bivona) Cosson, Compendium Florae Atlanticae 2: 53 (1887).

P. revelieri Jordan in Jordan and Fourreau, Icones ad Floram Europae 2: 38, t. 322 (1903).

EPITHET: *russoi*, after Giocchino Russo, abbot of Monte Casino and an amateur botanist interested in the Sicilian flora.

DESCRIPTION: Differs from subsp. *mascula* in having leaves pubescent beneath, lower leaves with 9 to 10 broadly elliptical to ovate leaflets. Flowering March to May. $2n = 20$.

DISTRIBUTION: Islands of the western Mediterranean, Greece, Corsica, Sardinia, and Sicily, growing on rocky limestone slopes and open woodland at altitudes of 400 to 1100 m (1320 to 3630 ft.).

COMMENT: This taxon was first recorded from Sicily as *Paeonia hyemalis, pumila, Rosae rubrae monoflorae* ("dwarf winter peony with a single rose-red flower") in Cupani's *Hortus Catholicus* (1696, p. 169) and later illustrated by an engraving in his *Pamphyton Siculum* (1713). The most beautiful of our many collections of this taxon is from Corsica (Carte JJH8706035); it has purplish leaves and stems and dark cyclamen-pink petals. This plant grows well in the open garden and flowers freely. Despite its distribution, it does not appear to be especially tender; however, it is possible that reported plants thriving in cold regions are not actually this subspecies but one of the other entities that have been given this name in the past. It is difficult to resolve this problem as no holotypes exist for these reported plants. See Figures 20, 21, 22.

P. mascula subsp. *atlantica* (Cosson) Greuter & Burdet in Wildenowia 12 (2): 198 (1982).

P. corallina var. *atlantica* Cosson, Compendium Florae Atlanticae 2: 54 (1883–1887).

P. russi var. *coriacea* (Boissier) Cosson ex Battandier & Trabut, Flore de l'Algerie 18 (1888), pro parte.

P. algeriensis Chabert in Bulletin de la Société botanique de France 36: 18 (1889).

P. atlantica Kralik ex Trabut in Bulletin de la Société botanique de France 62 (1889), nom. nud.

P. coriacea var. *atlantica* (Cosson) F. C. Stern in Journal of the Royal Horticultural Society 68: 128 (1943).

P. corallina subsp. *atlantica* (Cosson) Maire, Flore de l'Afrique du Nord 11: 30 (1964).

EPITHET: *atlantica*, "from the Atlas Mountains" of Algeria.

DESCRIPTION: Differs from subsp. *mascula* in having leaves pubescent on the lower surface and pubescent petioles. Flower color rose-pink. Flowering April to June. $2n = 20$.

DISTRIBUTION: Algeria, in the Atlas Mountains, growing in open woodland, on riverbanks, and on shrubby and rocky slopes at altitudes from 1200 to 2200 m (3960 to 7280 ft.).

COMMENT: Subspecies *atlantica* is very rare in gardens, and it is uncommon though not truly rare in the wild (as is true of most of the Mediterranean peonies). It will survive in a hot, sunny garden, protected against summer rain. We reintroduced this taxon to cultivation in 1991 (JJH910653).

P. mascula subsp. *hellenica* Tzanoudakis, Cytotaxonomic Study of the Genus *Paeonia* in Greece, p. 36 (1977).

EPITHET: *hellenica*, "Greek."

DESCRIPTION: Differs from subsp. *mascula* and subsp. *russoi* in having larger, white flowers. See Figure 20.

Key to the varieties of *P. mascula* subsp. *hellenica*
Leaves glabrous or pilose beneath, 9–13 leaflets with a length to breadth ratio of 1 to 1.25–1.7 . . . . var. *hellenica*
Leaves strongly pilose beneath, 11–21 leaflets with a length to breadth ratio of 2 to 2.4 . . . . var. *icarica*

P. mascula subsp. *hellenica* var. *hellenica*

DESCRIPTION: Stem to 60 cm (2 ft.) tall, glabrous. Lower leaves basically biternate, with 9–21 leaflets, obovate, broadly obovate or elliptic and shortly acuminate, twice or less than twice as long as broad, 1–3 of the leaflets sometimes deeply divided into similar segments; leaves grayish green above, glaucous beneath,

Figure 21. *Paeonia mascula* leaves: (top) subsp. *arietina*, (bottom) subsp. *russoi*.

Paeonia mascula subsp. *russoi*

Figure 22. Engraving of *Paeonia mascula* subsp. *russoi* in *Pamphyton Siculum* (Cupani 1713).

glabrous or pilose; terminal leaflets attenuate into a shortly decurrent petiolule. Flower 10–13 cm (4–5 in.) across. Petals five to seven obovate to obovate-orbicular, white. Filaments purplish red. Carpels one to five, usually three, long-tomentose. Style 8–10 × 2 mm; stigmatic area 2 mm broad, circinate from near the base. Flowering April to May. 2*n* = 20. This variety differs from var. *icarica* in having less pilose leaves and secondary top leaflets not divided.

DISTRIBUTION: Central Greece (Attica and Euboea); the Peloponnese (Lakonia), and Andros in the Cyclades, growing in open woodland, especially fir forests, and on rocky slopes at altitudes from 600 to 1200 mm (1880 to 3960 ft.).

COMMENT: We collected this taxon at three localities: on the Peloponnese (Mt. Taygetos JJH9005113); in Euboea (Mt. Dirfis JJH9005240); and on the island of Andros (Mt. Kouvara JJH9005287). These three collections vary slightly in the shape and size of both leaves and flowers. See Figure 23.

P. mascula subsp. hellenica var. icarica

(Tzanoudakis) Stearn in Stearn and Davis, Peonies of Greece 96 (1984).

P. folio subtus incano, flore albo vel pallido Cupani, Hortus Catholicus 169 (1696).

P. flavescens C. Presl in Presl, Deliciae Pragenses, 5 (1822).

P. corallina var. *flavescens* (C. Presl) Gussone, Florae Siculae Prodromus 2: 28 (1828–1832).

P. mascula var. *flavescens* (C. Presl) Gurke in Richter, Plantae Europeae 2: 400 (1903).

P. mascula subsp. *icarica* Tzanoudakis, A Cytotaxonomic Study of the Genus *Paeonia* in Greece, p. 36 (1977).

EPITHET: *icarica*, "of Ikaria," an island in the Aegean Sea.

DESCRIPTION: Differs from var. *hellenica* in having leaves strongly pilose beneath, top leaflets divided into four to seven segments, and having 11–21 leaflets with a length-to-breadth ratio of 2–2.4:1, instead of 9–13 leaflets with a length-to-breadth ratio of 1.25–1.7 to 1 in var. *hellenica*. Flowering April to May. 2*n* = 20.

DISTRIBUTION: Islands of Samos and Ikaria in Greece, and on Sicily, at altitudes of 400 to 650 m (1320 to 2130 ft.), growing on schistose substrates, in moist shady places in fir forest, in mixed oak woodland, and on open rocky slopes.

COMMENT: Both varieties *hellenica* and *icarica* are uncommon in cultivation, but they grow and flower well, enjoying hot, well-drained sites. Variety *icarica* was reintroduced by us in 1989 (Ikaria, Mt. Atheras JJH8906342) and in 1991 (Mt. Atheras JJH9106007). These two collections are uniform. See Figure 23.

P. mascula subsp. bodurii N. Özhatay, Karaca Arboretum Magazine 3 (1): 21 (1995).

EPITHET: *bodurii*, after S. Bodur, the first collector of this plant and a keen gardener.

DESCRIPTION: Stem glabrous, purplish, striate, up to 80 cm (32 in.) tall. Lower leaves biternate with (7–) 9 (–11) leaflets; leaflets obovate, broadly elliptic or nearly orbicular, shortly acuminate, 9–19 × 5–11 cm (3.5–7.5 × 2–4.4 in.), terminal leaflets attenuate into a shortly decurrent petiole. Leaves glabrous, grayish-green above, glaucous beneath. Upper cauline leaves ternate, leaflets 6–13 × 6–9 cm (2.4–5 × 2.4–3.5 in.), shortly acuminate. Flowers 11–12 cm (4.4–4.75 in.) across. Petals five to seven, obovate, white, purplish at the base. Filaments dark purplish, 1–1.3 cm (ca. 0.5

Figure 23. *Paeonia mascula* subsp. *hellenica* leaves: (top) var. *icarica*, (bottom) var. *hellenica*.

Paeonia mascula subsp. *hellenica* var. *hellenica* (above) and var. *icarica* (below)

Paeonia mascula subsp. *bodurii*

Figure 24. *Paeonia mascula* leaves: (top) subsp. *mascula*, (bottom) subsp. *bodurii*.

in.); anthers pink or yellow. Carpels three or four, short very dense white tomentose. Fertile seeds dark purplish. Flowering April to May. $2n = 20$.

DISTRIBUTION: Northwestern Turkey around Canakkale, growing in open woodland, around rocks, on shrubby rocky slopes, and under oaks at altitudes of 400 to 850 m (1320 to 2790 ft.).

COMMENT: Differs from subsp. *hellenica* in having cauline leaves ternate with folioles simple; differs from subsp. *mascula*, subsp. *arietina*, and subsp. *russoi* in having large white flowers. We introduced this taxon to cultivation, having collected it in 1996 at three localities on the hills from Canakkale to Troy (JJH960532, JJH960548, JJH960570). Collected plants bloomed freely in our garden in spring 1997. The flowers are very similar to those of var. *hellenica*, but bigger, with large purple blotches in the center, making them quite showy. See Figures 20, 24.

P. mascula subsp. kesrouanensis (Thiébaut) J. J. Halda in Acta Musei Richnoviensis 4 (2): 29 (1997).

P. corallina var. *kesrouanensis* Thiébaut, Bulletin de la Société botanique de France 81: 114 (1934).

P. kesrouanensis Thiébaut, Flore Libano-Syrienne 1: 37 (1936).

P. turcica Davis & Cullen, Notes from the Edinburgh Royal Botanic Garden 26: 176 (1965).

EPITHET: *kesrouanensis*, "of Kesrouan," a village northeast of Beirut, Lebanon.

DESCRIPTION: Differs from subsp. *mascula* in having glabrous carpels and long stigma, coiled at the extreme apex; lower leaves with 9–14 elliptic-ovate leaflets, glabrous or pilose beneath, sometimes subglaucous. Flowers small, ca. 10 cm (4 in.) across. Petals red. Carpels one or two. Flowering March to May.

DISTRIBUTION: Syria, Lebanon, and Turkey (Boz Dag and Finike), growing on rocky limestone slopes, among shrubs and in open oak forest or steep black pine (*Pinus nigra*) forest, at altitudes of 500 to 2200 m (1650 to 7280 ft.).

COMMENT: We collected this taxon on Boz Dag (JJH890633) under the name *Paeonia turcica*, which is conspecific with subsp. *kesrouanensis*. It is uncommon in cultivation but grows and flowers well. Its range suggests trying it in the U.S. Southwest. It is a pretty garden subject, similar in appearance to typical *P. mascula*. See Figure 20.

7. P. daurica Andrews, Botanist's Repository 7: t. 486 (1807).

EPITHET: *daurica*, a misrendering of *taurica*, "of the Crimea."

Key to the subspecies of *P. daurica*
    Leaflets very broadly elliptical; flowers
      rose-red . . . . Subsp. *daurica*
    Leaflets more narrowly elliptical; flowers
      pink . . . . Subsp. *lagodechiana*

P. daurica subsp. daurica

P. triternata Pallas ex de Candolle, Prodromus Systematis Naturalis Regni Vegetabilis 1: 165 (1824), nom. illegit.

P. corallina Retzius in M. B. Fl. Taur.-Cauc. 2: 10 (1808).

P. corallina var. *triternata* (Pallas) Boissier, Flora Orientalis 1: 97 (1867).

P. triternata f. *coriifolia* Ruprecht, Flora Caucasica, ser. 7, 15 (2): 44 (1869).

P. corallina var. *pallasi* Huth in Botanische Jahrbücher 14: 267 (1891).

P. corallina subsp. *triternata* (Pallas) N. Busch, Flora Caucasus Critica 3 (3): 10 (1901).

P. corallina subsp. *triternata* var. *coriifolia* (Ruprecht) N. Busch, Flora Caucasus Critica 3 (3): 12 (1901).

P. mascula var. *triternata* (Boissier) Gurke in Richter, Plantae Europeae 2: 400 (1903).

P. corallina Grossheim, Flora Kavkaza 2: 91 (1930).

P. corallina var. *caucasica* Schipczinski in Notulae systematicae ex herbario horti botanici petropolitanae 2: 45 (1921).

P. caucasica (Schipczinski) Schipczinski in Komarov, Flora of the USSR 7: 28 (1937).

P. caucasica var. *viridifolia* Kemularia-Nathadze in Flora Gruzii 4: 6 (1948).

P. kavachensis Grossheim, Flora Kavkaza 4: 12 (1950), non Asnavour.

P. kavachensis var. *coriifolia* (Ruprecht) Grossheim, Flora Kavkaza 4: 12 (1950).

P. corallina var. *triternatiformis* Nyarady in Savulescu, Flora Reipublicae Socialisticae Romania 2: 403 (1953).

P. ruprechtiana Kemularia-Nathadze, Not. Syst. Geog. Inst. Bot. Tbiliss, Trudy Tbilisi Botanical Institute 21: 28 (1961).

DESCRIPTION: Stem to 70 cm (28 in.) tall, glabrous. Lower leaves biternate, rather thick; leaflets usually nine, very broadly elliptic to broadly ovate-elliptic,

Paeonia daurica

Figure 25. *Paeonia daurica*. Leaf and mature follicle.

obovate or almost orbicular, shortly subacuminate, rounded or truncate at apex, 5–9 × 4–6 cm (2–3.5 × 1.5–2.4 in.), occasionally with some of the leaflets divided into one or two smaller leaflets, undulate at margin and somewhat upcurved, deep green above, glaucous and usually glabrous below, the terminal leaflets slightly or distinctly stalked; petiolule 5–20 mm. Flowers 7.5–10 cm (3–4 in.) across. Petals five to eight, obovate-orbicular, rose-red. Filaments yellow (purplish in Turkish plants). Carpels two to four, long-tomentose. Style 8–9 mm; stigmatic area ca. 2 mm broad, circinate from base. Follicles 25 mm long. Flowering May to June. $2n = 10$.

DISTRIBUTION: Southeastern Europe, Crimea, Caucasus, and Turkey, growing in open woodland, mountain forest, rocky slopes, and subalpine meadows up to 2800 m (9190 ft.) elevation.

COMMENT: Our collections from Turkey (Karlik Tepe JJH8709226, Samsun JJH9106015) have almost orbicular leaflets, but in the Transcaucasian plants (Osten JJH720712, Fist JJH720833, Soci JJH650715) all the leaflets are somewhat pointed. This is a vigorous, long-lived plant in suitable garden conditions. Some writers have treated this entity as a subspecies of *Paeonia mascula*; however, its globular seeds place it with *P. daurica*. See Figure 25.

P. daurica subsp. *lagodechiana* (Kemularia-Nathadze) J. J. Halda in Acta Musei Richnoviensis 4 (2): 29 (1997).

P. lagodechiana Kemularia-Nathadze, Not. Syst. Geog. Inst. Bot. Tbiliss, Trudy Tbilisi Botanical Institute 21: 33 (1961).

EPITHET: *lagodechiana*, "of Lagodechi" in Kachetia, Georgia.

DESCRIPTION: Differs from subsp. *daurica* in having glaucous, narrowly elliptic leaflets and broadly open pink flowers up 15 cm (6 in.) across. Flowering April to May. $2n = 10$.

DISTRIBUTION: Georgia, endemic in the area of Lagodechi, Kachetia, growing in open woodland, brushy slopes, and thickets.

COMMENT: This is a distinct and very showy plant, recently introduced by us (Lagodechi JJH720840, JJH840610). All individuals from this population are uniform. They grow well in an open site and flower freely.

8. *P. coriacea* Boissier, Elenchus Plantarum novarum 7 (1838).

P. corallina var. *coriacea* (Boissier) Cosson, Compendium Florae Atlanticae 2: 53 (1886).
P. corallina subsp. *coriacea* var. *maroccana* Pau & Font-Quer ex Jahandiez & Maire, Catalogue des Plantes du Maroc 2: 240 (1932).
P. corallina var. *russi* (Bivona) Webb, Iter. Hisp. 80 (1838), non Bivona.
P. coriacea var. *maroccana* (Pau & Font Quer) A. M. Romo in Journal of the Linnean Society, London, Botany 108 (3): 207 (1992).
EPITHET: *coriacea*, "leathery."

DESCRIPTION: Stem to 60 cm (2 ft.) tall, glabrous. Lower leaves biternate, but some of the 9 leaflets are bifurcated to give 14–16 leaflets; leaflets broadly elliptic, lanceolate to ovate, mostly acute, cuneate to widely cuneate or almost rounded at the base, the laterals practically sessile, glabrous and green above, glaucous and glabrous beneath. Flowers 7–15 cm (2.75–6 in.) across. Petals obovate, rose. Stamens 15–20 mm long, filaments red, anthers yellow. Carpels two, glabrous. Follicles 40–50 mm long. Flowering March to May. $2n = 20$.

DISTRIBUTION: Southern Spain and Morocco, growing on rocky slopes, in open woodland, and on mountain meadows at altitudes of 700 to 2200 m (2310 to 7280 ft.).

COMMENT: We have grown two different clones: one from the Spanish Sierra Nevada near Mulahacen (JJH8406112) with large, pale rose flowers and acute leaflets; and another from the Djebel Toubkal of Morocco (JJH850734) with smaller, darker flowers and much bigger leaflets. *Paeonia coriacea* is a vigorous, long-lived plant if given a hot, sunny site and good drainage. See Figure 26.

9. *P. corsica* Sieber ex Tausch in Flora 11: 86 (1828).

P. corallina var. *leiocarpa* Cosson, Notes sur quelques Plantes de France 2: 50 (1850).
P. cambessedesii (Willkomm) Willkomm in Willkomm & Lange, Prodromus Florae Hispanicae 3: 976 (1880), in obs., and Willkomm, Illustrationes Florae Hispanicae 1: 104, t. 65A (1883).
P. corallina Retzius, sec. Amo y Mora, Flora Fanerogamica de la Peninsula Iberica 6: 745 (1873), non Retzius.

Figure 26. Leaves of *Paeonia broteroi* (top) and *P. coriacea* (bottom).

Figure 27. *Paeonia corsica*. Leaf and mature follicle.

Paeonia corsica

P. corallina var. *cambessedesii* Willkomm, in Österreichische botanische Zeitschrift 25: 113 (1875).

P. corallina var. *corsica* (Sieber) Cosson, Compendium Florae Atlanticae 2: 53 (1886).

P. corallina f. *corsica* (Sieber) Rouy & Foucaud, Flore
de France 1: 144 (1893).

P. corallina var. *fructibus glabris* Cambessedes, Enumeratio Plantarum quas in Insulis Balearibus collegit J. Cambessedes 33 (1827).

P. officinalis subsp. *corallina* var. *corsica* (Sieber) Fiori
& Paoletti, Flora Analitica d'Italia 1: 527 (1898).

P. mascula var. *corsica* (Sieber) Gurke in Richter, Plantae Europeae 401 (1903), pro parte.

P. russi var. *leiocarpa* (Cosson) F. C. Stern in Journal
of the Royal Horticultural Society 68: 126 (1943).

P. mascula subsp. *cambessedesii* (Willkomm) O. Bolos
& Vigo in Butlleti de la Institucio Catalana d'Historia Natural, Seccio de Botanica, 38 (1): 65 (1974).

EPITHET: *corsica*, "of Corsica."

DESCRIPTION: Stem to 50 cm (20 in.) tall, glabrous.
Leaves coriaceous, regularly disposed along the stem,
decreasing in size towards the apex, 7.5–25 cm (3–10
in.) long; lower leaves biternate. Petiole up to 11 cm
(4.4 in.) long. Leaflets entire, from lanceolate to ovate,
sometimes elliptic, apex subacute to acute, 4–10 × 2–5
cm (1.5–4 × 0.75–2 in.), dark green and glabrous
above, with impressed veins, purple or pale green
flushed with purple and glabrous and with veins raised
below. Flowers 6–10 cm (2.4–4 in.) across. Petals
broadly obovate, deep rose. Stamens 10–17 mm long,
filaments red, anthers 3–4.5 mm long, yellow. Carpels
five to eight, glabrous, purple. Follicles 60 mm long.
Flowering March to April. 2n = 10.

DISTRIBUTION: Balearic Islands, central and southern Corsica, and northern Sardinia, growing in dry
stony places and open woodland.

COMMENT: One of the most charming peonies, this
species was introduced into cultivation in 1896 from
Majorca by a Miss Geoghegan of Dublin. It is now
widely grown under its more familiar synonym *Paeonia cambessedesii. Paeonia corsica*, however, is a much
older name and must therefore be accepted as valid.
Because it is small enough to maintain in a pot, it is a
popular alpine-house subject. Although the flowers,
soft pink flushed deep rose, are quite beautiful, the
foliage is perhaps even more so—the upper surfaces of
the leaves are overlain with a blue-silver bloom, while
the lower surfaces remain deep wine-red throughout
the growing season. Even the seedpods are exceptionally ornamental with their brilliant magenta inner

membrane, dark blue fertile seeds, and bright red
infertile ones.

Our plants originating from Majorca (JJH840728)
are particularly vigorous, with bright rose flowers. This
species is more demanding in the garden than many
others, requiring a warm site protected from summer
rain. Some overhead cover in winter is also desirable,
because the flowers appear very early and can be spoiled
by rain. Our plants grow under a south-facing balcony,
together with *Paeonia brownii* and its subspecies *californica. Paeonia corsica* is easily raised from seed, which
can be obtained through the exchanges of alpine gardening societies and is likely to be true because the flowers appear so early; seedlings often flower after two seasons of growth. Because of the paucity of pollinators
during its flowering time in northern areas, this species
is best pollinated by hand. See Figure 27.

10. *P. broteroi* Boissier & Reuter, Diagnoses
Plantarum novarum Hispanicarum 4 (1842).

P. broteroi var. *ovatifolia* Boissier & Reuter, Diagnoses
Plantarum novarum Hispanicarum 4 (1842).

P. corallina var. *broteroi* (Boissier & Reuter) Cosson,
Compendium Florae Atlanticae 2: 53 (1866).

P. corallina f. *broteroi* (Boissier & Reuter) Voss in Vil-
morin's Blumengarten 39 (1894).

P. lobata Desfontaines ex Boissier, Voyage Botanique
dans le Midi de l'Espagne 2: 14 (1839), nom. illegit.

P. lusitanica Miller, Gardeners Dictionary, no. 8
(1768).

P. lusitanica var. *ovatifolia* (Boissier & Reuter) Sampaio, Lista das Especies Representadas no Herbario
Portugues 53 (1913).

P. mascula var. *broteroi* (Boissier & Reuter) Gurke in
Richter, Plantae Europeae 2: 401 (1903).

P. mascula var. *ovatifolia* (Boissier & Reuter) Gurke in
Richter, Plantae Europeae 2: 401 (1903).

P. mascula var. *lusitanica* (Miller) Sampaio, in Annales Scientificos da Academia Polytecnica do
Porto 4–6: 8 (1909–1911).

P. mascula var. *ovatifolia* (Boissier & Reuter) Sampaio,
in Annales Scientificos da Academia Polytecnica
do Porto 4–6: 8 (1909–1911).

P. officinalis Linnaeus, sec. Brotero, Flora Lusitanica,
2: 299 (1804), non Linnaeus emend. Willdenow.

P. officinalis var. *lobata* (Desfontaines) Webb, Iter.
Hisp. 80 (1831).

P. officinalis var. *lusitanica* (Miller) Martyn, Gardeners
Dictionary, 2: 1, no. 2 (1807).

EPITHET: *broteroi*, after Felix de Silva Avellar Brotero (1744–1828), a Portuguese botanist.

DESCRIPTION: Stem glabrous, to 50 cm (20 in.) tall. Leaves shining green; lower leaves biternate, divided into (9–) 17 (–20) narrowly elliptical, glabrous segments 9–10 × 2.8–3.5 cm (3.5–4 × 1–1.4 in.), with the terminal leaflets and sometimes the laterals deeply divided into two or three segments; upper leaves biternate, with leaflets undivided; leaflets sessile, elliptic, attenuated to the acute apex and to the cuneate base, or broadly elliptic, subacute at the apex and widely cuneate at the base, glabrous, shining green above, glaucous beneath; petiole more or less terete. Flowers 8–10 cm (3–4 in.) across. Petals broadly obovate, red. Stamens 20–25 mm long, filaments and anthers yellow. Carpels two to four, densely white tomentose. Follicles 30–40 mm long. Flowering April to May. $2n = 10$.

DISTRIBUTION: Southern and western Spain and Portugal, growing on limestone slopes and in open woodland at altitudes of 800 to 2000 m (2640 to 6600 ft.).

COMMENT: We collected this taxon twice: in the Sierra de Guadarrama of Spain (JJH840755) and in Coimbra district, Portugal (JJH840823). The two collections are similar. This species is well established in cultivation. See Figure 26.

Subsection *Anomalae*

Subsection *Anomalae* (Kemularia-Nathadze ex Uspenskaja) J. J. Halda in Acta Musei Richnoviensis 4 (2): 26 (1997).

Paeonia section *Paeonia* series *Anomalae* Kemularia-Nathadze ex Uspenskaja in Byulleten Moskovskogo Obshchestva Ispytatelei Prirody, Biology, 92 (3): 84 (1987).

Paeonia section *Sternia* series *Anomalae* and series *Hybridae* Kemularia-Nathadze, Not. Syst. Geog. Inst. Bot. Tbiliss, Trudy Tbilisi Botanical Institute 21: 35 (1961), nom. nud.

Paeonia subsection *Dissectifoliae* group *Anomala* Stern, A Study of the Genus *Paeonia*, p. 112 (1946), nom. nud.

DESCRIPTION: Leaf segments laciniate; leaflets lanceolate.

TYPE SPECIES: *P. anomala* Linnaeus.

11. *P. anomala* Linnaeus, Mantissa altera 247 (1771).

P. fructibus quinque glabris patentibus Gmelin, Flora Sibirica 4: 184, t. 72 (1769).

P. quinquecapsularis Pallas, Reise durch verschiedene Provinzen des russischen Reichs 3: 316 (1776), nom. tant.

P. laciniata Pallas, Flora Rossica 1 (2): 85 (1788).

P. sibirica Pallas, Flora Rossica 1 (2): 85 (1788).

P. anomala var. *nudicarpa* Huth in Botanische Jahrbücher 14: 269 (1891);.

P. anomala var. *typica* Regel, Reisen in Den Süden von Ost-Sibirien 1: 125 (1861).

P. anomala var. *angustifolia* I. M. Krasnoborov in Sistematiceskie Zametki po Materialam Gerbarii Imeni P. N. Krylov pri Tomskom Gosudarstvennom Universitete 85 (27): 2 (1974, published 1975).

EPITHET: *anomala*, "irregular."

Key to the subspecies of *P. anomala*
 Carpels and follicles glabrous . . . .
 . . . . Subsp. *anomala*
 Carpels tomentose; follicles villous . . . .
 . . . . Subsp. *hybrida*

P. anomala subsp. *anomala*

DESCRIPTION: Stem glabrous, up to 1 m (3 ft.) tall. Leaves biternate, but the leaflets are pinnatisect with numerous narrow deltoid or subulate segments, some of which are deeply two- or three-lobed; segments narrow-oblong, acuminate-attenuate at the apex, up to 10 × 2 cm (4 × 0.75 in.), dark green above with minute bristles along the veins, glabrous and glaucous below. Flowers pink to crimson, 7–9 cm (2.75–3.5 in.) across. Petals obovate, apex truncate, margins undulate. Stamens 15 mm long, filaments and anthers yellow. Carpels three to five, ca. 2 cm (0.75 in.) long, glabrous. Follicles 17 × 15 mm long. Flowering April to July. $2n = 10$.

DISTRIBUTION: Northeastern Russia, parts of the Ural Mountains, and southern Siberia, growing on mountainous and subalpine slopes, in open woodland, along rivers, and in pastures at 400 to 3200 m (1,320 to 10,270 ft.).

COMMENT: This species has probably been in cultivation for many years; it grows well in the open garden and flowers freely. It is reported to grow well in gardens where winter temperatures reach −30°C (−22°F) or colder. We collected this taxon many times from

Paeonia broteroi

Paeonia anomala

Figure 28. *Paeonia anomala* leaves: (top) subsp. *anomala*, (bottom) subsp. *hybrida*.

throughout its range. The illustrated plant is from the Baikal area (E Sayan JJH650731). See Figure 28.

P. anomala subsp. ***hybrida*** (Pallas) J. J. Halda, Acta Musei Richnoviensis 4 (2): 29 (1997).

P. hybrida Pallas, Flora Rossica 2: 94 (1788).

P. intermedia C. A. Meyer ex Ledebour, Flora Altaica 2: 277 (1830).

P. officinalis Linnaeus sec. Falk, Beitrage 2: 198 (1785–1786).

P. anomala var. *hybrida* f. *intermedia* Trautvetter, Schrenk in Bulletin de la Société Imperiale des Naturalistes de Moscow 33: 88 (1860).

P. anomala var. *typica* Huth in Botanische Jahrbücher 14: 268 (1891), non Regel (1861).

P. hybrida var. *intermedia* (C. A. Meyer ex Ledebour) Krylov and var. *typica*, Flora Altaja 1: 47 (1901).

P. anomala subsp. *intermedia* (C. A. Meyer ex Ledebour) Fedtschenko, Flora Zapadnovo Tjan-Shana 1: 103 (1904).

P. intermedia subsp. *pamiroalaica* Ovczinnikov in Flora Tadzikskoj USSR 4: 531 (1975).

EPITHET: *hybridus,* "mixed, not true."

DESCRIPTION: Differs from subsp. *anomala* in having tomentose carpels and later villous follicles.

DISTRIBUTION: Finnish Lapland, northern Russia, the Altai Mountains, and Turkestan in Central Asia.

COMMENT: This very hardy plant is amenable to cultivation in northern gardens. We collected it many times (offering seed under the name *Paeonia intermedia*) in different parts of its range; each area has a slightly different form. The illustrated plant comes from the Vanch valley in the central Pamirs (JJH720854). See Figure 28.

12. *P. veitchii* Lynch in Gardeners' Chronicle, ser. 3 (46): 2 (1909).

P. anomala Maximowicz in Acta Horti Petropolitani 11: 34 (1890).

P. beresowskii Komarov in Notulae systematicae ex herbario horti botanici petropolitanae 2: 5 (1921).

P. veitchii var. *beresowski* (Komarov) Schipczinski in Notulae systematicae ex herbario horti botanici petropolitanae 2: 46 (1921).

P. veitchii var. *purpurea* Schipczinski in Notulae systematicae ex herbario horti botanici petropolitanae 2: 46 (1921).

P. veitchii var. *leiocarpa* W. T. Wang & S. H. Wang in Flora Reipublicae Populis Sinicae 27: 56 (1979).

EPITHET: *veitchii,* after Sir Harry James Veitch (1840–1924), English horticulturist and nurseryman.

Key to the subspecies of *P. veitchii*
    Flowers small, 5–9 cm (2–3.5 in.) across . . . . Subsp. *veitchii*
    Flowers much larger, 10–18 cm (4–7 in.) across in mature plants . . . . Subsp. *altaica*

P. veitchii subsp. *veitchii*

DESCRIPTION: Stem to 60 cm (2 ft.) tall, glabrous. Leaves biternate; leaflets deeply cut into two to four segments, which are deeply lobed (rarely entire), segments and lobes oblong-elliptic, long-attenuated to the acuminate apex, 5–15 mm broad, dark green above with minute bristles along the midrib and main nerves, pale to glaucous-green and glabrous below. Flowers usually two or more to a stem, 5–9 cm (2–3.5 in.) across, all shades of magenta. Petals broadly obovate-cuneate, apex truncate or emarginate. Stamens 12–17 mm long, filaments pink, anthers yellow. Carpels two to five, usually four, densely tomentose. Follicles 15 × 12 mm, strongly recurved at maturity. Flowering May to July. $2n = 10$.

DISTRIBUTION: China, in the provinces of Gansu, Shanxi, Shaanxi, Sichuan, and Qinghai, growing in open woodland, on rocky slopes, mountain pastures, and river banks at altitudes of 800 to 3600 m (2,640 to 11,810 ft.).

COMMENT: This species differs from the most closely related species, *Paeonia anomala,* in having several much smaller flowers on a stem and densely tomentose carpels; in addition, the flowers appear about a month later than those of *P. anomala.* We collected this species many times in Sichuan and Gansu. The plant illustrated is from Sichuan (Minya Gonka JJH820815). See Figure 29.

Key to the varieties of *P. veitchii* subsp. *veitchii*
    Leaf midrib and main nerves with minute bristles . . . . Var. *veitchii*
    Leaf midrib and main nerves with bristly hairs . . . . Var. *woodwardii*

P. veitchii subsp. *veitchii* var. *veitchii*

Description as above.

Paeonia veitchii

Figure 29. *Paeonia veitchii* leaves: (top) subsp. *veitchii*, (bottom) subsp. *altaica*.

P. veitchii subsp. *veitchii* var. *woodwardii* (Stapf ex Cox) F. C. Stern in Journal of the Royal Horticultural Society 68: 130 (1943).

P. woodwardii Stapf ex Cox, The Plant Introductions by Reginald Farrer, p. 43 (1930).

DESCRIPTION: Differs from var. *veitchii* by having bristly hairs on the midrib and nerves of both surfaces of leaves and on the petioles and petiolules. Flowering May to June. $2n = 10$.

DISTRIBUTION: China, in the provinces of Sichuan and Gansu, growing in open woodland at altitudes of 600 to 2400 m (1880 to 7870 ft.).

COMMENT: We collected this taxon in two localities: Sichuan (Pali Shan JJH820985) and Gansu (Sinlo Shan JJH821037). It is widely grown in gardens, especially in the British Isles, but many seed-grown plants cultivated under this name may be hybrids.

P. veitchii subsp. *altaica* (K. M. Dai & T. H. Ying) J. J. Halda, Acta Musei Richnoviensis 4 (2): 29 (1997).

P. altaica K. M. Dai & T. H. Ying in Bulletin of Botanical Research 10 (4): 33 (1990).

DESCRIPTION: Differs from subsp. *veitchii* in having broader leaflets, bigger (10–18 cm or 4–7 in. across) emarginate flowers, and subglobose, smaller pollen grains. Flowering April to June. $2n = 10$.

DISTRIBUTION: China, province of Xinjiang, growing in open woodland and on rocky slopes at altitudes of 1300 to 1500 m (4290 to 4950 ft.).

COMMENT: We collected this taxon only once (Aletai area JJH9610215); the seed was not ripe, so we obtained several plants, which bloomed for the first time in 1997. They have very large flowers (15 cm or 6 in. across) with tiny anthers (ca. 5 mm long). It promises to be an unusual, first-rate garden plant. See Figure 29.

Subsection *Obovatae*

Subsection *Obovatae* Komarov ex Uspenskaja in Byulleten Moskovskogo Obschchestva Ispytatelei Prirody, Biology, 92 (3): 84 (1987).

Paeonia series *Obovatae* Komarov in Flora of the USSR 7: 26 (1937), nom. inval.

Paeonia group *Obovata* Stern, A Study of the Genus *Paeonia*, p. 21 (1946).

DESCRIPTION: Flowers rose or white; leaf segments entire, orbiculate or oval.

TYPE SPECIES: *P. obovata* Maximowicz.

13. *P. obovata* Maximowicz, Primitiae Florae Amurensis 29 (1859).

EPITHET: *obovata*, "obovate," referring to the shape of the terminal leaflet.

Key to the subspecies of *P. obovata*
Larger, to 70 cm (28 in.), leaves sparsely villow below, flowers as for species . . . . Subp. *obovata*
Smaller, to 50 cm (20 in.), leaves glabrous, flower white . . . . Subsp. *japonica*

P. obovata subsp. *obovata*

P. oreogeton S. Moore in Journal of the Linnean Society, London, Botany 17: 376 (1879).

P. obovata var. *typica* Makino in Botanical Magazine, Tokyo, 12: 302 (1898).

P. wittmanniana Lindley, sec. Finet & Gagnepain, Bulletin de la Société botanique de France, p. 525 (1904).

P. obovata var. *amurensis* Schipczinski and var. *australis* Schipczinski in Notulae systematicae ex herbario horti botanici petropolitanae 2: 44 (1921).

P. vernalis Mandl in Botanikai Közlemenyek 19: 90 (1921).

P. obovata var. *alba* Saunders in National Horticulture Magazine (Washington) 13: 227 (1934).

Key to the varieties of *P. obovata* subsp. *obovata*
Leaf underside glaucous with sparse hairs, flowers white or rose pink . . . . . . Var. *obovata*
Leaf underside villous, flowers usually white . . . . Var. *willmottiae*

P. obovata subsp. *obovata* var. *obovata*

DESCRIPTION: Stem 40–70 cm (16–28 in.) tall, glabrous. Lower leaves biternate; leaflets unequal, terminal usually obovate, laterals broadly oval or oblong, all shortly acuminate at the apex, cuneate or widely cuneate at the base, mostly 5–12 × 3.5–7 cm (2–4.75 × 1.4–2.75 in.), in fruit up to 15 × 9 cm (6 × 3.5 in.), thinly papery, dark green and glabrous above, glaucous and sparsely villous below. Flowers white to rose-purple, up to 8 cm (3 in.) across. Stamens 17 mm long, filaments white or rose, anthers yellow. Carpels two or three, glabrous, 2 cm (0.75 in.) long, attenuated, stigma conspicuous, 5 mm across. Follicles 30–35 mm long. $2n = 10, 20$.

DISTRIBUTION: Russia, in the Far East (Udsk, Ussuri, and Zee-Buryat.), the Amur region, Manchuria,

Paeonia obovata subsp. *obovata*, two color forms

Figure 30. Leaves of *Paeonia mairei* (top) and *P. obovata* (bottom).

the Kurile Islands, and Sakhalin; Korea; China, provinces of Shanxi, Sichuan, and Yunnan; and Japan. It grows in oak, birch, and mixed forests, on open slopes, and on riverbanks up to 2000 m (6600 ft.) elevation.

COMMENT: This charming plant occupies a large range, but is uniform over its vast area. An interesting character is the presence of both diploids and tetraploids in wild populations. Populations from Russian Manchuria and Amur have smaller, deep pink flowers, as seen in the lower plant in the illustration (Sichote Alin JJH740725); populations from Sakhalin are pinkish creamy or white, like the upper plant in the plate (Mt. Lopatina JJH740913). In cultivation the most common form is a white-flowered one that probably originated in Japan, described as var. *alba* Saunders. The species grows well in half shade in any well-drained position. See Figure 30.

P. obovata subsp. **obovata** var. **willmottiae** (Stapf) Stern in Journal of the Royal Horticultural Society 68: 128 (1943).

P. willmottiae Stapf in Curtis's Botanical Magazine, t. 8667 (1916).

EPITHET: *willmottiae*, after noted gardener Ellen Ann Willmott (1860–1934).

DESCRIPTION: Differs from variety *obovata* in being more robust, with villous leaf underside and earlier, white flowers with more attenuated carpels. Flowering April to June. $2n = 10, 20$.

DISTRIBUTION: China, in Hubei and Shaanxi provinces, growing in mixed forest, among rocks, and on shrubby slopes at altitudes up to 2600 m (8530 ft.).

COMMENT: We collected this taxon twice: in Shaanxi (Tabei Shan JJH8708233) and Hubei (JJH8708315). Both forms are vigorous and bloom about two weeks earlier than var. *obovata*. This variety needs half shade and good drainage.

P. obovata subsp. **japonica** (Makino) J. J. Halda, Acta Musei Richnoviensis 4 (2): 30 (1997).

P. obovata var. *japonica* Makino in Botanical Magazine, Tokyo, 12: 302 (1898).

P. japonica (Makino) Miyabe & Takeda in Gardeners' Chronicle, ser. 3 (48): 366 (1910).

P. obovata var. *glabra* Makino in Journal of Japanese Botany 5 (9): 33 (1928).

DESCRIPTION: Differs from subsp. *obovata* in being smaller and in having glabrous leaves and white flowers with short stigmas. Flowering April to May. $2n = 10$.

DISTRIBUTION: Russia, on Sakhalin; and Japan, on Hokkaido. It grows on streambanks and in open woodland at low elevations.

COMMENT: We collected this taxon in both its areas; plants from the Novosachalinsk area (JJH650733) and those from the Sapporo area (JJH850812) are very similar, with small white flowers. As has happened with other genera introduced from Japan, the name "japonica" has been loosely applied to garden peonies; the *RHS Dictionary of Gardening* (1992) notes that plants grown under this name may be a form of *Paeonia suffruticosa*.

14. P. mairei Léveillé in Bulletin de geographie botanique (Le Mans) 25: 42 (1915).

P. bifurcata Schipczinski in Notulae systematicae ex herbario horti botanici petropolitanae 1: 3 (1920).

P. oxypetala Handel-Mazzetti in Anzeiger der Akademie der Wissenschaften in Wien 57: 265 (1920).

P. mairei f. *oxypetala* (Handel-Mazzetti) Fang, Acta Phytotaxonomica Sinica 7 (4): 307 (1958).

EPITHET: *mairei*, after René Charles Joseph Ernest Maire (1878–1949), a French botanist.

DESCRIPTION: Stem to 1 m (3 ft.) tall, glabrous. Lower leaves biternate, sometimes with lateral leaflets bifurcate; leaflets elliptic or obovate-elliptic, cuneate to long-cuneate at the base, long-acuminate to caudate at the apex, $12–20 \times 3–8$ cm ($4.75–8 \times 1–3$ in.), dark green above, paler below, glabrous, of thin papery texture. Flowers 8–12 cm (3–4.75 in.) across. Petals rose, obovate to obovate-elliptic, rounded at the apex. Stamens 15–20 mm long, filaments purplish, anthers yellow. Carpels 2–2.5 cm (0.75–1 in.) long, conical in the lower part, attenuated upward to the stigma, densely covered with a silky tomentum of short golden-brown hairs, or glabrous. Flowering May to June. $2n = 10$.

DISTRIBUTION: China, in provinces of Yunnan and Sichuan, growing in open woodland and on riverbanks at altitudes from 800 to 3500 m (2640 to 11,480 ft.).

COMMENT: Our collections from Sichuan (Minya Gonka JJH9008045) and Yunnan (Haba Shan JJH9007004, Beima Shan JJH90070015) are more or less uniform, a bit variable in color of corolla, ranging from pale pink to rose-pink. This taxon is not very common in cultivation, but it grows and flowers well in rather shady sites. The plant known as forma *oxypetala* is only a variant with acute, dentate petals; such individuals co-occur with the type. See Figure 30.

Paeonia obovata subsp. *japonica*

Paeonia mairei

Section *Tenuifoliae*

Section *Tenuifoliae* (Stern ex Uspenskaja) J. J. Halda, Acta Musei Richnoviensis 4 (2): 27 (1997).

Paeonia section *Paeonia* series *Tenuifolia* Stern ex Uspenskaja in Byulleten Moskovskogo Obschchestva Ispytatelei Prirody, Biology, 92 (3): 84 (1987).

Paeonia subgenus *Paeonia* section *Palearcticae* subsection *Tenuifoliae* (Stern ex Uspenskaja) J. J. Halda, Acta Musei Richnoviensis 4 (2): 27 (1997).
DESCRIPTION: Leaf segments pinnatisect.
TYPE SPECIES: *P. tenuifolia* Linnaeus.

15. *P. tenuifolia* Linnaeus, Systema naturae, ed.10, 2: 1079 (1759).

P. multifida Gueldenstein, Reisen 2: 19 (1791).

P. tenuifolia var. *plena* Sweet, British Flower Garden 7: 345 (1836).

P. tenuifolia var. *flore pleno* Lemaire in Flore des Serres 4: 308 (1848).

P. hybrida Janka, in Österreichische botanische Zeitschrift 5: 60 (1855), non Pallas.

P. tenuifolia var. *laterecta* Neilreich Augzahl, Nachter 70 (1876).

P. tenuifolia var. *hybrida* (Pallas) Lipsky, Fl. Ciscauc. 235 (1889–1892).

P. tenuifolia var. *parviflora* Huth in Botanische Jahrbücher 14: 271 (1891).

P. tenuifolia var. *typica* Schipczinski in Notulae systematicae ex herbario horti botanici petropolitanae 2: 46 (1921).

P. lithophila Kotov in Journal de l'Institut Botanique de l'Académie des Sciences d'Ukraine 13 (3): 49 (1956).
EPITHET: *tenuifoliate*, "with fine leaves."

Key to the subspecies of *P. tenuifolia*
    Leaflets very narrow, only 2–5 mm wide . . . . .
    . . . . Subsp. *tenuifolia*
    Leaflets broader to 15 mm wide . . . .
    . . . . Subsp. *biebersteiniana*

P. tenuifolia subsp. *tenuifolia*

DESCRIPTION: Stem 15–70 cm (6–28 in.) tall, glabrous, densely leafy with the flower resting as if it were on the foliage. Leaves divided into many linear segments, which are less than 5 mm wide, glabrous above, pubescent beneath; lower leaves divided on a biternate pattern, but the leaflets completely dissected and lobed tripinnately into very numerous finely linear segments,

0.5–2 mm wide, subacute to obtuse at the apex, glabrous and dark green above, glaucous below; petioles and petiolules glabrous. Flowers ca. 6–8 cm (2.4–3 in.) across. Petals deep crimson, oblanceolate or obcuneate to obovate with the apex rounded to truncate or even emarginate. Stamens ca. 15 mm long, filaments, anthers and pollen yellow. Carpels usually three, densely coarse-tomentose. Follicles two or three, ca. 20 mm long, tomentose. $2n = 10$.

DISTRIBUTION: Eurasia, from southeastern Europe through Turkey, southwestern Russia, and Ukraine to the Caucasus, growing on dry grassy slopes, open steppe, among limestone rocks, or in open woodland at altitudes of 50 to 2100 m (160 to 6890 ft.).

COMMENT: We have collected this species many times throughout virtually its entire range. Most of our collections are uniform; only plants from the western Caucasus differ, in that they are smaller in all their parts. The plants illustrated are from Georgia (Kartli JJH6607112). Given good drainage, it is an excellent garden plant, as adaptable as its large range suggests. The double-flowered form is more common than the typical form in gardens. It has been grown at least since the 19th century. This peony has a reputation for being difficult to grow, but not all gardeners find it so. The flower buds seem particularly susceptible to frost damage, but situating the plants with light overhead cover may mitigate this. Interestingly, a correspondent in Ottawa, Canada, reports that *Paeonia tenuifolia* (both single and double forms) is very successful there, where the winter minimum temperature is −30°C (−22°F) or colder. The cold temperatures and reliable snow cover keep the plants dormant until it is safe for them to emerge. In cold northern climates, it does best in full sun and rich soil. See Figure 31.

P. tenuifolia subsp. *biebersteiniana* (Ruprecht) J. J. Halda, Acta Musei Richnoviensis 4 (2): 29 (1997).

P. biebersteiniana Ruprecht, Flora Caucasica, p. 47 (1869).

P. tenuifolia Ruprecht, Flora Caucasica, p. 47 (1869).

P. tenuifolia var. *hybrida* Lipsky, Fl. Ciscauc. 235 (1889–1892).

P. tenuifolia var. *biebersteiniana* (Ruprecht) N. Busch, Flora Caucasus Critica 3 (3): 9 (1901–1903).

P. carthalinica N. Ketzchoweli, Osn. tipy rast. Gruzii 20 (1935).
EPITHET: *biebersteiniana*, after Friedrich August Marschall von Bieberstein (1768–1826), a German botanist.

Figure 31. *Paeonia tenuifolia* leaves: (top) subsp. *biebersteiniana*, (bottom) subsp. *tenuifolia*.

Paeonia tenuifolia

DESCRIPTION: Differs from subsp. *tenuifolia* in having leaflets much broader, up to 1.5 cm (0.6 in.) wide. Flowering April to May. $2n = 10$.

DISTRIBUTION: Northern Caucasus, where it is endemic in the Stavropol Territory, growing on dry, open slopes among shrubs.

COMMENT: Our plants are from the Pjatigorsk area (JJH650734); they are vigorous and quite hardy. See Figure 31.

Section *Emodi*

Section *Emodi* (Stern) J. J. Halda, Acta Musei Richnoviensis 5 (1): 1–48.
Paeonia section *Paeonia* subsection *Foliolatae* group *Lactiflora* Stern, A Study of the Genus *Paeonia* (1946).
DESCRIPTION: Flowers white, solitary (may be more), leaves biternate.
TYPE SPECIES: *P. emodi* Wallich ex Royle.

16. *P. emodi* Wallich ex Royle, Illustrations of the Botany of the Himalayan Mountains 57 (1834).

P. anomala var. *emodi* (Wallich) Huth in Botanische Jahrbücher 14: 269 (1891).
P. officinalis Linnaeus, sec. Hooker f. & Thomson, Flora Indica 60 (1855), non Linnaeus emend. Willdenow.
P. emodi f. *glabrata* (Hooker f. & Thomson) H. Hara in H. Hara, A. O. Charter, and H. J. Williams, An Enumeration of Flowering Plants of Nepal 2: 23 (1979).
EPITHET: *Emodos*, according to Ptolemy (ca. 150 C.E.), is the easternmost part of the Central Asian ranges—Paropamisos, Imaos, and Emodos.

Key to the subspecies of *P. emodi*
    Flowers larger 7.5–10 cm (3–4 in.) across; leaflets entire or divided into two or three terminal leaflets . . . . Subsp. *emodi*
    Flowers smaller, up to 7.5 cm (3 in.) across, leaflets more deeply lobed and toothed . . . . . .
    . . . . Subsp. *sterniana*

P. emodi subsp. *emodi*

DESCRIPTION: Stem 30–100 cm (12–40 in.) tall, glabrous, light green, bearing one to four flowers. Lower leaves biternate; leaflets usually decurrent and conflu-ent at the base, entire or often deeply divided into two, or the terminal leaflet into three segments, leaflets or segments elliptic, narrowed to the base and to the acuminate apex, 10–18 × 1.5–6 cm (4–7 × 0.6–2.4 in.), dark green and glabrous above, only minutely puberulous along the veins, sometimes lighter green and glabrous below. Flowers 8–13 cm (3–5 in.) across. Petals obovate, shiny white. Stamens 15–20 mm long, filaments and anthers yellow. Carpel usually one, densely hispid, hairs yellowish. Follicles 25–27 mm long. Flowering April to June. $2n = 10$.

DISTRIBUTION: India in the western Himalayas and Kashmir; Pakistan in the Chitral region. It grows in open woodland, on riverbanks, and in subalpine pastures at 1200 to 3200 m (3,960 to 10,270 ft.).

COMMENT: We collected this plant several times in Pakistan and India. The plant illustrated is a very vigorous form, almost 1 m (3 ft.) tall, from the Garwhal Himal (JJH820736). Others, from Chitral (JJH840945, JJH8409102), are much shorter, with smaller flowers. There are reports of forms that do well in the cold climate of eastern Canada, but lower-elevation collections may prove less cold-hardy. Some writers identify a variety or forma *glabrata*; however, I have found that glabrous individuals are frequent in every population examined. See Figure 32.

P. emodi subsp. *sterniana* (H. R. Fletcher) J. J. Halda, Acta Musei Richnoviensis 4 (2): 29 (1997).

P. sterniana H. R. Fletcher in Journal of the Horticultural Society (London) 134: 327 (1959).
EPITHET: *sterniana*, after Frederick Claude Stern (1884–1967), an enthusiastic collector and gardener.
DESCRIPTION: Differs from subsp. *emodi* in having smaller, solitary flowers (up to 8 cm or 3 in. across), and deeply lobed and toothed leaflets. Flowering April to June.
DISTRIBUTION: Southeastern Tibet in Kongbo, Tamnyen, and Gyala, growing among shrubs in stony places, and in shady oak forest, at altitudes from 2600 to 3000 m (8530 to 9900 ft.).
COMMENT: I know this plant only from a herbarium specimen. It is very closely related to *Paeonia emodi*. Very interesting are Fletcher's (1959) notes:

On 21 July 1938, Mr. Frank Ludlow and Dr. George Taylor were collecting in the Tsangpo Valley in the Kongbo Province of South-East Tibet. Near Gyala, under the dense shade of *Quercus ilex* forest, they stopped for a wayside lunch and soon

Figure 32. *Paeonia emodi* leaves: (top) subsp. *emodi*, (bottom) subsp. *sterniana*.

Paeonia emodi

realized that they were sitting on a fruiting peony. The fruits were green and immature and although flowers were not to be seen, the natives affirmed that these were white. Two months later, when Ludlow and Taylor returned to collect mature fruits, they found that all the seeds had been shed. Nine years later, on 18 April 1947, Mr. Ludlow and Colonel H. H. Elliot, at a place called Tamnyen, found the plant again, just coming into flower, and a week later, 24 April, they gathered beautiful flowering specimens at the spot where Ludlow and Taylor had found it originally in 1938. As the natives had affirmed, the flowers were white. Finally, at Tamnyen, on 5 August 1947, Ludlow and Elliot collected mature indigo-blue seeds from the bright red capsules.

See Figure 32.

Section *Flavonia*

Section *Flavonia* Kemularia-Nathadze, Not. Syst. Geog. Inst. Bot. Tbiliss, Trudy Tbilisi Botanical Institute 21: 18, 22 (1961).

Paeonia section *Flavonia* Kemularia-Nathadze and series *Macrophyllae* Kemularia-Nathadze and series *Wittmannianae* Stern ex Kemularia-Nathadze, Not. Syst. Geog. Inst. Bot. Tbiliss, Trudy Tbilisi Botanical Institute 21: 18, 22 (1961).

Paeonia section *Palearcticae* Huth emend. Uspenskaja subsection *Flavonia* (Kemularia-Nathadze) Uspenskaja in Byulleten Moskovskogo Obshchestva Ispytatelei Prirody, Biology, 92 (3): 83 (1987)

Paeonia series *Corallinae* Komarov in Flora of the USSR 7: 28 (1937).

Paeonia subsection *Foliolatae* group *Wittmanniana* Stern, A Study of the Genus *Paeonia*, p. 53 (1946).

DESCRIPTION: Flowers yellow, creamy or whitish yellow. Leaf segments entire.

TYPE SPECIES: *P. wittmanniana* Hartwiss ex Lindley.

Key to section *Flavonia*
   Staminodial disc fleshy, lobate, ca. 4 mm; diploid . . . . 17. *P. mlokosewitschii*
   Staminodial disc tiny, ca. 1 mm; tetraploid . . . . 18. *P. wittmanniana*

17. *P. mlokosewitschii* Lomakin in Trudy Tiflisskogo Botaniceskogo Sada 2: 282 (1897).

P. mlokosiewiczi N. Busch, Flora Caucasus Critica 3 (3): 14 (1901).

EPITHET: *mlokosewitschii*, after J. L. Mlokosewicz, an enthusiastic plant collector in the Caucasus.

DESCRIPTION: Stem to 1.3 m (4 ft.) tall, glabrous. Lower leaves biternate; leaflets broadly oblong or oval to ovate or obovate, apex subacute to rounded and shortly cuspidate, 6–15 × 3.5–7 cm (2.4–6 × 1.4–2.75 in.), dark green and glabrous above, glaucous and sparsely pubescent with very short curved hairs below. Flowers 8–14 cm (3–5.5 in.) across. Petals slightly concave, broadly obovate, yellow. Stamens up to 25 mm long, filaments and anthers yellow. Carpels two to four, densely tomentose, stigma light pink or yellow. Follicles 30–50 mm long. Flowering April to June. $2n = 10$.

DISTRIBUTION: Georgia, in eastern Transcaucasia, and Lagodechi in Kachetia, growing among rocks and on open slopes in oak-beech forests.

COMMENT: We often collected this charming species. The plant illustrated is from Ninigora (JJH630835) and is more compact than the typical form, with large, good yellow flowers. A deservedly popular and first-rate garden plant, in cultivation since 1902, it grows and flowers well in any well-drained position. Gardeners in Britain especially cherish it, but they complain that its early flowers are fleeting and easily damaged by spring rains. It hybridizes readily in the garden, and many plants in cultivation under this name turn out to be hybrids, often recognizable by anomalous foliage characteristics and pink-flushed flowers. Hybrid populations also occur in the wild (see "Natural Hybrids"). See Figure 33.

18. *P. wittmanniana* Hartwiss ex Lindley in Botanical Register 32: 9 (1846).

P. wittmanniana subsp. *tomentosa* (Lomakin) N. Busch, Flora Caucasus Critica 3 (3): 14 (1901), pro parte.

P. wittmanniana var. *tomentosa* Lomakin in Trudy Tiflisskogo Botaniceskogo Sada 1: 30 (1895), pro parte.

P. abchasica Misczenko ex Grossheim, Flora Kavkaza 2: 92 (1930).

P. corallina var. *wittmanniana* Albov, Prodromus Florae Colchicae 14 (1895).

P. macrophylla Lomakin, sec. Saunders in National Horticulture Magazine (Washington 13: 224 (1934), pro parte, non (Albov) Lomakin.

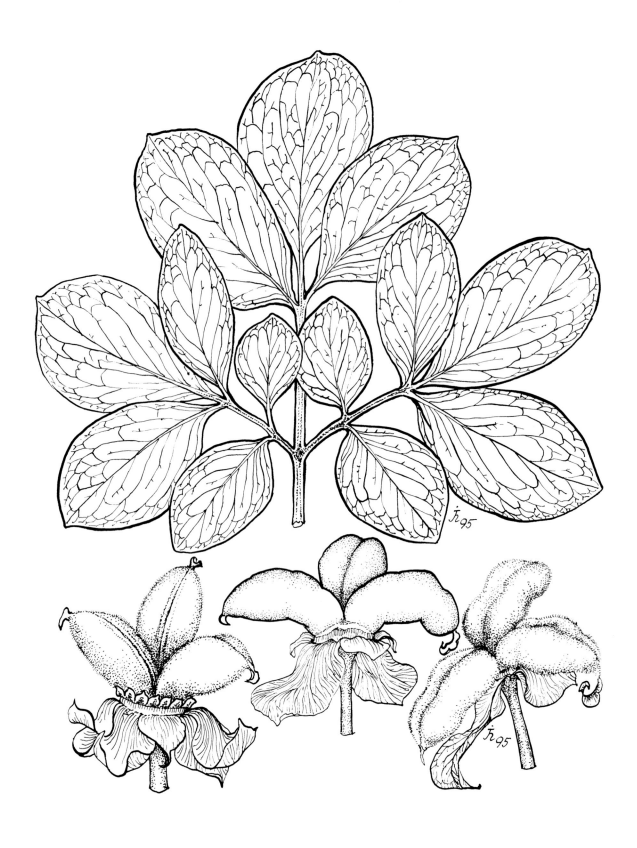

Figure 33. *Paeonia mlokosewitschii* leaf (top). Mature follicles (bottom, left to right): *P. mlokosewitschii*,
P. wittmanniana subsp. *macrophylla*, *P. wittmanniana* subsp. *wittmanniana*.

Paeonia mlokosewitschii

Figure 34. Leaves of *Paeonia wittmanniana*: (top) subsp. *wittmanniana*, (bottom) subsp. *macrophylla*.

P. wittmanniana Buhse, Aufzahl. Transcauc. Pers. Pfl. p. 8 (1860).

P. mlokosewitschii Grossheim, Opredetel rastenii kavkasa, p. 44 (1949).

P. wittmanniana var. *tomentosa* Lomakin in Trudy Tiflisskogo Botaniceskogo Sada 2: 283 (1897).

P. tomentosa (Lomakin) Busch ex Grossheim, Flora Kavkaza 2: 91 (1930).

EPITHET: *wittmanniana*, after C. Wittmann, a plant collector in Caucasus and a keen gardener in the late 19th century.

Key to the subspecies of *P. wittmanniana*
Leaflets to 18 × 12 cm (7 × 4.75 in.) . . . .
. . . . Subsp. *wittmanniana*
Leaflets larger than above, up to 25 × 15 cm
(10 × 6 in.) . . . . Subsp. *macrophylla*

P. wittmanniana subsp. *wittmanniana*

DESCRIPTION: Stem glabrous, to 1.5 m (5 ft.) tall. Lower leaves biternate. Leaflets broadly ovate or broadly elliptic to oblong-oval, acutely cuneate to obliquely truncate at the base, apex bluntly acute to acuminate, 8–18 × 4.5–12 cm (3–7 × 1.75–4.75 in.), glabrous and shining dark green above, lighter green or glaucescent below, with scattered long white hairs especially dense along the veins, petioles with long scattered hairs at the apex. Flowers 10–13 cm (4–5 in.) across, bowl-shaped. Petals concave, orbicular to broadly obovate, concave, creamy to sulfur yellow. Stamens 20 mm long, filaments red, up to 1 cm (0.4 in.) long; anthers golden yellow, 1 cm (0.4 in.) long. Carpels usually two to four, green, glabrous, stigma crimson. Follicles 30–40 mm long. Flowering April to June. $2n = 20$.

DISTRIBUTION: Georgia, in western, eastern, and southern Transcaucasia; Iran, in the Elburz Mountains and Iranian Kurdistan; Armenia, in Kurdistan; and Turkey, in northeastern Anatolia and Kurdistan. It grows in open mixed or beech montane forest at altitudes from 800 m (2640 ft.), rising to alpine meadows and open rocky slopes at 3000 m (9900 ft.).

COMMENT: This species was first described by N. de Hartwiss from cultivated material received by the Royal Horticultural Society in October 1842, collected in Abkhazia and sent to de Hartwiss by Count M. Voroncov. Our collections (about 30) cover the entire range of this species. Our most beautiful form is a pale yellow-flowering plant from Adzharia (Agara JJH660537). *Paeonia wittmanniana* has been wide-spread in cultivation for at least a hundred years; it grows and flowers well in the open garden. See Figures 33, 34.

P. wittmanniana subsp. *macrophylla* (Albov) J. J. Halda, Acta Musei Richnoviensis 4 (2): 30 (1997).

P. wittmanniana Steven in Bulletin de la Société Imperiale des Naturalistes de Moscow 3: 275 (1848)

P. wittmanniana var. *macrophylla* (Albov) N. Busch ex Grossheim, Flora Kavkaza 2: 91 (1930).

P. corallina var. *wittmanniana* f. *macrophylla* Albov, Prodromus Florae Colchicae 15 (1895).

P. wittmanniana f. *macrophylla* (Albov) N. Busch, Flora Caucasus Critica 3: 3 (1901–1903).

P. wittmanniana var. *nudicarpa* Schipczinski in Notulae systematicae ex herbario horti botanici petropolitanae 2: 44 (1921).

P. wittmanniana Kolakovsky, Fl. Abch. 2: 121 (1939).

P. macrophylla (N. Albov) Lomakin in Trudy Tiflissakago Botaniceskogo Sada, 2: 282 (1897).

P. steveniana (Steven) Kemularia-Nathadze, Not. Syst. Geog. Inst. Bot. Tbiliss, Trudy Tbilisi Botanical Institute 21: 20 (1961).

EPITHET: *macrophylla*, "large leaves."

DESCRIPTION: Differs from subsp. *wittmanniana* in having the larger leaflets and glabrous carpels. Flowering April to July. $2n = 20$.

DISTRIBUTION: Georgia, in Adzharia, and the western Caucasus, growing in montane forest and open subalpine meadows up to 3200 m (10,270 ft.).

COMMENT: This taxon is common throughout Transcaucasia and is typified by leaflets up to 25 × 16 cm (10 × 6.4 in.) in size, as well as by creamy flowers with glabrous carpels. The pictured plant is from Imeretia (Bachmaro JJH660609). *Paeonia wittmanniana* var. *nudicarpa* is described as lacking tomentose fruit, but this common phenotype seems well within the range of normal variation for *P. wittmanniana* subsp. *macrophylla*. See Figures 33, 34.

Subgenus *Albiflora*

Subgenus *Albiflora* (Salm-Dyck) J. J. Halda, Acta Musei Richnoviensis 5 (1): 1–48. 1998.

Paeonia section *Albiflora* Salm-Dyck, Hortus Dyckensis, 366 (1834).

Paeonia section *Albiflora* Salm-Dyck ex Uspenskaja in Byulleten Moskovskogo Obschchestva Ispytatelei Prirody, Biology, 92 (3): 83 (1987).

Paeonia wittmanniana

6x

Figure 35. *Paeonia lactiflora*: (top) leaf; (bottom left) mature follicle; (bottom right) leaf margin.

Paeonia section *Paeon* subsection *Foliolatae* group *Lactiflora* Stern, A Study of the Genus *Paeonia* (1946).

DESCRIPTION: Leaf edge cartilaginous, more or less dentate, gradually acute toward apex.

TYPE SPECIES: *P. lactiflora* Pallas.

19. *P. lactiflora* Pallas, Reise durch verschiedene Provinzen des russischen Reichs 3: 286 (1776).

P. albiflora Pallas, Flora Rossica 1 (2): 92, t. 84 (1788).

P. albiflora var. *edulis* (Salisbury) Pursh in Donn, Hortus Cantabrigiensis, ed. 8: 177 (1815).

P. albiflora var. *fragrans* Sabine in Transactions of the Horticultural Society, London, 2: 278, t. 18 (1816).

P. albiflora var. *hirta* Regel, Reisen in Den Süden von Ost-Sibirien 1: 125 (1861).

P. albiflora var. *hortensis* Makino in Journal of Japanese Botany 5 (9): 34 (1928).

P. albiflora var. *purpurea* Korshinsky in Acta Horti Petropolitani 12: 302 (1892).

P. albiflora var. *spontanea* Makino in Journal of Japanese Botany 5 (9): 33 (1928).

P. albiflora var. *typica* Huth in Botanische Jahrbücher 14: 265 (1891).

P. albiflora var. *whitleyi* Anderson, Transactions of the Linnean Society, London, 12: 259 (1818).

P. edulis Salisbury, Paradisus Londinensis, t. 78 (1805).

P. edulis reevesiana Paxton, Paxton's Magazine of Botany 1: 197 (1841).

P. edulis var. *sinensis* Sims in Botanical Magazine, Tokyo, t. 1768 (1815).

P. fragrans (Sabine) Redoute, Choix Flora 13: 106 (1827).

P. lactea Pallas, Reise durch verschiedene Provinzen des russischen Reichs 3: 321 (1776).

P. lobata Pallas, Reise durch verschiedene Provinzen des russischen Reichs 2: 553 (1773).

P. officinalis Linnaeus sec. Thunberg, Flora Japonica 230 (1784), pro parte.

P. officinalis Loureiro, Flora Cochinensis 1: 343 (1790), non Linnaeus emend. Willdenow.

P. reevesiana (Paxton) Loudon, Supplement to Hortus Britannicus, 601 (1850).

P. whitleyi (Anderson) Hort. ex Garden 36: 8 (1889).

P. albiflora var. *trichocarpa* Bunge, Enumeratio Plantarum 3 (1834).

P. lactiflora var. *trichocarpa* (Bunge) F. C. Stern in Journal of the Royal Horticultural Society 68: 129 (1943).

P. yui Fang, Acta Phytotaxonomica Sinica 7 (4): 321 (1958).

P. lactiflora f. *nuda* (Nakai) M. Kitagawa, Neolineamenta Florae Manshuricae 302 (1979).

P. lactiflora f. *pilosella* (Nakai) M. Kitagawa, Neolineamenta Florae Manshuricae 303 (1979).

EPITHET: *lactiflora*, "milky-white flowered."

DESCRIPTION: Stem to 80 cm (32 in.) tall, glabrous, light green flushed with red, bearing two or more flowers. Lower leaves biternate; leaflets entire or occasionally lobed, elliptic to lanceolate, cuneate at the base, apex acute to acuminate, more rarely rounded and apiculate, dark green and glabrous above except for minute hairs along the nerves, lighter green and glabrous or with short hairs along the nerves below, margin papillose and rough to the touch. Flower 7–10 cm (2.75–4 in.) across, sweetly scented. Petals obovate, white. Stamens ca. 15 mm long, filaments creamy yellow, anthers yellow. Carpels four or five, glabrous, stigma pink. Follicles ca. 20 mm long. Flowering April to June. $2n = 10$.

DISTRIBUTION: Northeast China, Inner Mongolia, and Shanxi, and in Tibet; Mongolia; far eastern Russia and central Siberia (Dahuria). It grows on dry, open, stony slopes, in open woodland, and on riverbanks up to 2400 m (7870 ft.).

COMMENT: We collected this species many times in Siberia, Mongolia, and China; the illustrated plant is from Transbaikalia (Daurskij chrebet JJH660893), where this species is quite common, with many color forms from pure white to rose-pink. *Paeonia lactiflora* and its cultivars have been widespread in cultivation in China and Japan for at least a thousand years, and this species is an important ancestor of modern garden hybrids. This plant is vigorous and long-lived in practically any conditions. Roots of this species are very useful as understocks for grafting woody peonies.

This species is extremely variable. I found that many of the names mentioned in the synonymy have been applied to the kinds of individual variations that are relatively common in almost any wild population, co-occurring with the typical phase. For this reason, I do not distinguish them as subspecies or varieties. See Figure 35.

Subgenus *Onaepia*

Subgenus *Onaepia* (Lindley) Lynch in Journal of the Royal Horticultural Society, new ser. 12: 432, 433 (1890).

Paeonia lactiflora

DESCRIPTION: Stems herbaceous, annual; petals coriaceous, not larger or only slightly larger than sepals; disc produced as fleshy lobes at the base of carpels.

TYPE SPECIES: *P. brownii* Douglas ex Hooker.

20. *P. brownii* Douglas ex Hooker, Flora Boreali-Americana 1: 27 (1829).

EPITHET: *brownii*, after Robert Brown (1773–1858), an American botanist.

Key to the subspecies of *P. brownii*
> Stems up to 38 cm (15 in.); petals shorter
> than sepals . . . . Subsp. *brownii*
> Stems up to 1 m (3 ft.); petals as long or
> slightly longer than sepals . . Subsp. *californica*

***P. brownii* subsp. *brownii* Douglas. Journal Trav. N. Amer. 192, 197, 201, 268 (1914). J. J. Halda, stat. nov.**

DESCRIPTION: Stems 24–50 cm (10–20 in.) tall, glabrous. Leaves five to seven, biternate, with the leaflets shortly stalked; leaflets divided to the base into three segments; segments deeply divided, three- or four-lobed; lobes entire or lobulate or toothed, apex of lobes rounded to obtuse, with a very short point; leaflets fleshy, with a strong marginal vein, glabrous, dark green above and glaucous below. Flower subglobose, not opening widely, 2–3 cm (0.75–1.1 in.) across. Sepals broad ovate to suborbicular, 10–22 × 10–21 mm, coriaceous. Petals broad oval to suborbicular, 9–14 × 7–16 mm, thinly coriaceous, dark maroon. Stamens ca. 10 mm long, filaments yellowish, anthers yellow. Carpels five, glabrous; disc surrounding the base of the carpels fleshy, lobed, 2.5–3 mm high. Follicles erect or slightly spreading, 25–30 × 15–18 mm. Flowering April to June. $2n = 10$.

DISTRIBUTION: Western United States in northern California, Idaho, Nevada, Oregon, Utah, Washington, and Wyoming, growing in sagebrush communities on high desert, in montane ponderosa pine (*Pinus ponderosa*) forest, and on rocky slopes.

COMMENT: Growing at high elevations, this plant experiences a very long, fairly cold winter (often with little or no snow cover) and a short spring growing season, when it blooms and ripens its seeds. The hot, dry summer of the semiarid West then causes a long dormancy. Our plants came from the Wenatchee Mountains in Washington State, from property of Coleman

Leuthy (JJH9605113), where there is a large population of vigorous plants, and from eastern Oregon (Painted Hills area JJH880534), where it grows together with *Lewisia rediviva*, *Pediocactus simpsonii* var. *robustior*, and *Fritillaria pudica*. The two populations are uniform in size, shape, and color of flowers. This species seems much more reluctant to germinate than Old World species. See Figure 36.

***P. brownii* subsp. *californica* (Nuttall ex Torrey & Gray) J. J. Halda, Acta Musei Richnoviensis 4 (2): 31 (1997).**

P. californica Nuttall ex Torrey & Gray, Flora of North
America 1: 41 (1838).
P. brownii var. *californica* (Nuttall ex Torrey & Gray)
Lynch in Journal of the Royal Horticultural Society 12: 433 (1890).

EPITHET: *californica*, "of California."

DESCRIPTION: Differs from subsp. *brownii* in being taller, in having leaves less divided and lobed; leaf segments and lobes acute at apex; petals 17–20 mm long, as long as or slightly longer than the inner sepals, which are 15–19 mm long. Flowering April to May. $2n = 10$.

DISTRIBUTION: United States, in central and southern California, growing on semidesert hills at low elevations.

COMMENT: Our plants originally came from the foothills of the Sierra Nevada (Silver Hills JJH8906111), where infrequent populations exist. Both var. *brownii* and var. *californica* are vigorous and long-lived plants in suitable conditions. They need a summer drought period and can be treated much like summer-dormant dryland bulbs. They need a moist fall, winter, and spring, but after dying back they are sensitive to moisture. They prefer a heavier soil, which when dry acts like concrete and protects the roots against moisture loss. Our garden plants set seed and the seedlings grow readily in situ. Subspecies *californica* is a bit more ornamental than subsp. *brownii*, but both are necessary members of any representative collection. With its demanding cultural requirements and small, dull flowers, this is certainly a species of interest only to the serious collector. Seed may usually be obtained from collectors and botanic gardens in its native region; germination tends to be much less predictable than it is for other species. See Figure 36.

Figure 36. *Paeonia brownii* leaves: (top) subsp. *californica*, (bottom) subsp. *brownii*.

Paeonia brownii subsp. *brownii*

Paeonia brownii subsp. *californica*

Subgenus *Moutan*

Subgenus *Moutan* (de Candolle) Seringe, Flora des Jardins 3: 187 (1849).

Section *Moutan* de Candolle, Prodromus Systematis Naturalis Regni Vegetabilis 1: 65 (1824).

Section *Suffruticosae* Salm-Dyck, Hortus Dyckensis, 365, 366 (1834).

Section *Moutania* Reichenbach, Repert. Herb. s. Nom. Gen. Pl. 191 (1841).

Section *Palearcticae* subsection *Fruticosae* Huth in Botanische Jahrbücher 14: 272 (1891).

Section *Mutan* Ascherson & Graebner, Synopsis der Mitteleuropaischen Flora 5 (2): 558 (1923).

Section *Moutan* (de Candolle) Reichenbach in Moessler, Handbuch der Gewachskunde, ed. 2 (1): 40 (1827), pro gen.

DESCRIPTION: Stems woody, perennial, petals thin, much longer than sepals.

TYPE SPECIES: *P. suffruticosa* Andrews.

Key to subgenus *Moutan*

1a. Staminodial disc as a thin leathery sheath, covering whole carpels in full bloom; lower leaves bipinnate [Section *Moutan*] 2

1b. Staminodial disc as conspicuous fleshy lobes around the base of carpels, reaching up to one-third of carpels; lower leaves biternate, deeply lobed or toothed [Section *Delavayanae*] 3

2a. Carpels completely enveloped by staminodial disc . . . . 21. *P. suffruticosa*

2b. Carpels enveloped only up to one-half to two-thirds . . . . 22. *P. decomposita*

3a. Calyx of five leathery greenish sepals with a conspicuous involucre of 8–12 green bracts; flowers red . . . . 23. *P. delavayi*

3b. Calyx without an involucre; bracts and sepals five to seven, the outer one to four more or less foliaceous, the innermost rounded and sepal-like 4

4a. Segments and lobes of leaves 17–30 mm wide; flowers up 9 cm (3.5 in.) across, yellow or yellow with reddish blotch at base . . . . 24. *P. lutea*

4b. Segments and lobes of leaves 5–10 mm wide, upper segments wider; flowers smaller, red, white, or yellow . . . . 25. *P. potaninii*

Section *Moutan*

Section *Moutan*

Paeonia section *Moutan* subsection *Vaginatae* F. C. Stern in A Study of the Genus *Paeonia*, p. l. (1946).

Paeonia section *Moutan* series *Suffruticosae* Kemularia-Nathadze, Not. Syst. Geog. Inst. Bot. Tbiliss, Trudy Tbilisi Botanical Institute 21: 14 (1961), nom. inval.

DESCRIPTION: Disc produced as a thin leathery sheath which at first completely envelops the carpels; lower leaves bipinnate with some hairs on lower surface; pinnae entire or more often palmately two- or three-lobed.

TYPE SPECIES: *P. suffruticosa* Andrews.

21. *P. suffruticosa* Andrews, Botanists Repository 6: 373 (1804).

EPITHET: *suffruticosa*, "semiwoody."

Key to the subspecies of *P. suffruticosa*

The four subspecies are highly variable with multiple natural and manmade hybrids. See the discussion on "The *P. suffruticosa* Complex." This key is suitable for wild-collected materials, but cultivated materials are complex hybrids.

1a. Flowers of various colors, usually pink, red, rose, or purple, rarely white, single or double 2

1b. Flowers usually white, single (up to 10 petals) 3

2a. Leaflets ovate and sharply three-lobed, flowers variable single and double, unmarked; widespread and variable . . . . Subsp. *suffruticosa*

2b. Leaflets on wild plants ovate to circular with blunt lobes; flowers pale to rose-pink . . . . Subsp. *spontanea*

3a. Flowers pure white sometimes blushed pink in center; terminal leaflets usually with one to three lobes, plants form low shrubs . . . . Subsp. *ostii*

3b. Flowers with mostly obvious deep purple flares in center; terminal leaflets usually entire; plants form more upright shrubs . . . . Subsp. *rockii*

P. suffruticosa subsp. *suffruticosa*

P. arborea Donn, Hortus Cantabrigiensis, ed. 3, 102 (1804), nom. nud.

Figure 37. *Paeonia suffruticosa* subsp. *spontanea* leaves: (top) subsp. *spontanea*, (bottom) var. *qiui*.

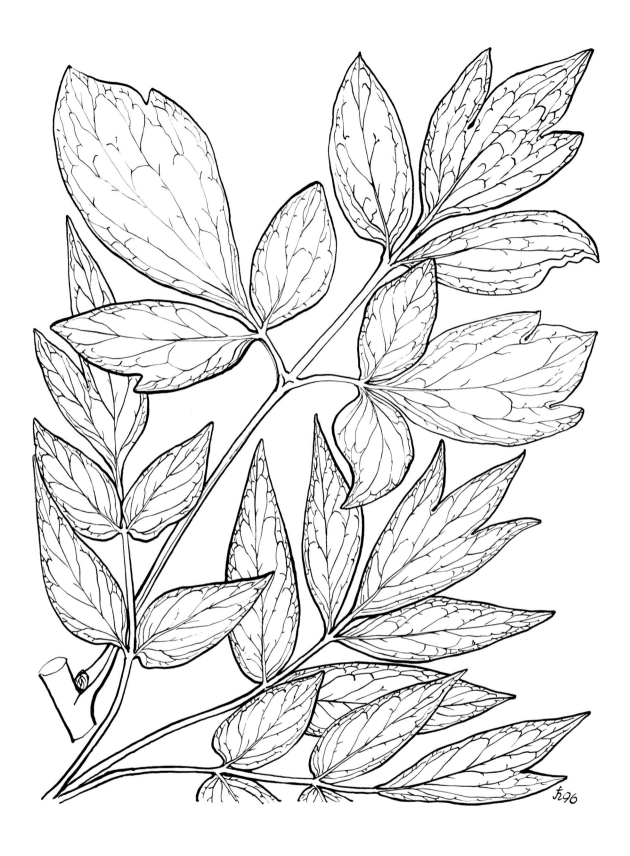

Figure 38. *Paeonia suffruticosa* leaves: (top) subsp. *suffruticosa*, (bottom) subsp. *ostii*.

Figure 39. *Paeonia suffruticosa* leaves: (top) subsp. *rockii*, (bottom) subsp. *rockii* var. *linyanshanii*.

Paeonia suffruticosa subsp. *suffruticosa*

P. suffruticosa var. *purpurea* Andrews, Botanist's Repository 7: 448 (1807).

P. moutan Sims, Curtis's Botanical Magazine 29: 1154 (1808).

P. arborea C. C. Gmelin, Hortus Magni Ducis Badensis Carlsruhanus 192 (1811).

P. chinensis Oken, Allgemeine Naturgeschichte fur alle Stande 3 (2): 1164 (1841) fide Merrill, Journal of the Arnold Arboretum 31: 282 (1950).

P. suffruticosa subsp. *atava* Bruehl, Annals of the Royal Botanic Garden Calcutta 5 (2): 114–115, t. 126 (1896).

P. decomposita Handel-Mazzetti, Acta Horti Gothoburg 13: 39 (1939).

P. yunnanensis Fang, Acta Phytotaxonomica Sinica 7 (4): 306, pl. 612 (1958).

DESCRIPTION: A shrub up to 2 m (6.5 ft.) tall; branches glabrous. Leaves bipinnate, usually with nine or sometimes more leaflets, ovate to broadly ovate, terminal leaflets usually deeply three-lobed, often also with a few shallow lobes, very rarely entire, tips of lobes acute, rachis and petiole more or less glabrous. Flowers single or double; petals white, pink, red, purple, or lilac, immaculate (rarely with a reddish-purple basal blotch). Flowering April to May. $2n = 10$.

DISTRIBUTION: China, in provinces of Shaanxi, and western Hubei, and in southeastern Tibet, growing in thickets and open woodland at altitudes from 800 to 1500 m (2640 to 4950 ft.).

COMMENT: This widespread and variable species comprises a number of entities that have been given specific rank at one time or another. It is not possible to associate all the garden cultivars of *Paeonia suffruticosa* with subspecies or varieties; no doubt some of them arose in Chinese gardens over the centuries during which these plants have been carefully cultivated. The evidence of Chinese paintings testifies to the esteem in which the moutan was traditionally held. Most cultivars of the modern "tree peony" grown in European gardens before World War II were seedlings and crosses of the first plants brought from Chinese gardens. After *P. lutea* was discovered and introduced at the end of the 19th century, it was hybridized with these garden moutans, resulting in the much wider range of colors found today. See Figure 38.

P. suffruticosa subsp. *spontanea* (Rehder) S. G. Haw & L. A. Lauener, Edinburgh Journal of Botany 47 (3): 278 (1990).

P. suffruticosa var. *spontanea* Rehder, Journal of the Arnold Arboretum 1: 193 (1920).

EPITHET: *spontanea*, "wild, natural."

DESCRIPTION: Leaves with nine leaflets, ovate or broadly ovate to more or less circular, usually rather bluntly lobed. Flowers single, rather small, purple, rose-pink, or rarely white, unblotched. Flowering April to June. $2n = 10$.

Key to the varieties of *P. suffruticosa* subsp.
    spontanea

1a.   Flowers pale to rose-pink or purple 2
1b.   Flowers white, single . . . . var. *jishanensis*
2a.   Leaflets ovate to broadly ovate to nearly circular, blunt on end . . . . var. *spontanea*
2b.   Leaflets ovate to rotundly ovate, terminal leaflet with three equal dentate divisions . . . . var. *qiui*

P. suffruticosa subsp. *spontanea* var. *spontanea*

DISTRIBUTION: China, in provinces of Shanxi and western Hubei, growing on open hills, among thickets, on rocky slopes, and in open woodland at altitudes up to 2400 m (7870 ft.).

COMMENT: Our collections from Shanxi include the illustrated plant (Wuigong Shan JJH90060024), with huge silky-pink flowers; one from Sichuan (Lao Shan JJH9209008) with rose-pink flowers; and one from Hubei (Winpa Shan JJH8407006) with pale pink flowers. These are to my knowledge the only wild collections of this taxon, which we found in its habitat after eight expeditions. We saw many cultivated plants in public gardens; most of them were double-flowered, but there were also many singles. See Figure 37.

P. suffruticosa subsp. *spontanea* var. *jishanensis* (T. Hong & W. Z. Zhao) J. J. Halda, Acta Musei Richnoviensis 4 (2): 30 (1997).

P. jishanensis T. Hong & W. Z. Zhao, in Bulletin of Botanical Research 12 (3): 225 (1992).

EPITHET: *jishanensis*, "from Jishan."

DESCRIPTION: Differs from variety *spontanea* in having white petals without petaloid stamens. Flowering April to May.

DISTRIBUTION: China, in Shanxi province (Jishan, Xiqiu), growing in forests, on slopes and among thickets at altitudes from 1200 to 1450 m (3960 to 4760 ft.).

COMMENT: To my knowledge, this taxon is not cultivated in the West.

P. suffruticosa subsp. ***spontanea*** var. ***qiui*** (Y. L. Pei & Hong) J. J. Halda, Acta Musei Richnoviensis 4 (2): 31 (1997).

P. qiui Y. L. Pei & Hong in Acta Phytotaxonomica Sinica 33 (1): 91 (1995).

EPITHET: *qiui*, after Qiu Jun-zhuan, recent Chinese botanist and collector.

DESCRIPTION: Differs from var. *spontanea* in having folioles ovate or ovate-rotund, entire; the terminal one with three equal divisions or dentate. Flowering April to May.

DISTRIBUTION: Hubei province (Shennongjia Shan, Sunbai Town), growing in thickets, on steep rocks, and in open woodland at altitudes from 1600 to 2100 m (5280 to 6890 ft.).

COMMENT: This variety is not in cultivation at present, as far as I have heard. It is to be hoped that the development of relations between Chinese botanical institutes and Western botanists and nursery people will soon lead to the introduction of this and other recently described peonies. See Figure 37.

P. suffruticosa subsp. ***ostii*** (T. Hong & J. X. Zhang) J. J. Halda, Acta Musei Richnoviensis 4 (2): 30 (1997).

P. ostii T. Hong & J. X. Zhang in Bulletin of Botanical Research 12 (3): 223 (1992).

EPITHET: *ostii*, after Gian Lupo Osti, Italian botanist.

DESCRIPTION: Differs from subsp. *rockii* in having narrowly ovate-lanceolate entire leaflets which are glabrous beneath. Terminal leaflets with one to three lobes. Petals mostly white, without purple basal blotch, but often suffused pink at base of petals; filaments, disc, and styles purplish red. Flowering April to May. $2n = 10$.

DISTRIBUTION: China, in provinces of Gansu (Liangdang), Henan (Songxian, Yangshan), Hunan (Longshan), and Shanxi (Meixian, Taibaishan), growing in thickets on slopes at altitudes from 800 to 1400 m (2640 to 4620 ft.).

COMMENT: This is another recently established Chinese taxon that has not yet been introduced in the West. The cultivar 'Fen Dan Bai' may be a hybrid or a selection of this subspecies. See Figure 38.

P. suffruticosa subsp. ***rockii*** S. G. Haw & L. A. Lauener, Edinburgh Journal of Botany 47 (3): 279 (1990).

P. suffruticosa sensu Stern, A Study of the Genus *Paeonia*, p. 40 (1946), pro parte and sensu Fang, Acta Phytotaxonomica Sinica 7 (4): 302 (1958), pro parte.

P. suffruticosa var. *papaveracea* sensu K. Y. Pan, Flora Reipublicae Popularis Sinicae (Beijing) 27: 45 (1979), non Kerner.

P. suffruticosa 'Rock's Variety' ('Joseph Rock') hort.

P. rockii (S. G. Haw & L. A. Lauener) T. Hong & J. J. Li in Bulletin of Botanical Research 12 (3): 227 (1992).

EPITHET: *rockii*, after Joseph Francis Charles Rock (1884–1962), botanist and collector.

Key to the varieties of *P. suffruticosa* subsp. *rockii*
1a.   Leaflets usually numerous 19–31 2
1b.   Leaflets fewer, 9–11 . . . . var. *yananensis*
2a.   Leaflets ovate, narrowly ovate or lanceolate, may be entire or with two to four lobes . . . . var. *rockii*
2b.   Leaflets lanceolate or narrowly ovate, entire . . . . var. *linyanshanii*

P. suffruticosa subsp. ***rockii*** var. ***rockii***

DESCRIPTION: Leaves more or less triternate or bipinnate to tripinnate, always with more than nine leaflets (usually 19–31, rarely as few as 11), leaflets ovate, narrowly ovate or lanceolate, acute, usually entire or sometimes two- to four-lobed. Flowers very large, single, with about 10 white petals blotched with deep purple at the base, the disc sheathing the carpels whitish, and the filaments purple only near the base, whitish toward the tip. Flowering April to June. $2n = 10$.

DISTRIBUTION: China, in provinces of Shanxi (Nan Wutai Shan), southeastern Gansu (Wang Jia Shan), northern Sichuan, and Qinghai, growing on open hills, rocky slopes, and among shrubs at altitudes up to 2800 m (9190 ft.).

COMMENT: We collected this taxon twice in Gansu, in the same area, the Wang Jia Shan. One collection (JJH87050016) has small purple blotches in center; the other, illustrated in this work (JJH87050022), has purplish leaves and huge flowers with bigger purple blotches on more or less crenate petals. According to information received from local residents, there are six or more nearby localities where similar plants grow, but we were not able to find them. A clone of this subspecies grown in Western gardens for more than a cen-

Paeonia suffruticosa subsp. *rockii*

tury is known as the cultivar 'Joseph Rock' or 'Rock's Variety'; it has always been much sought by gardeners and has commanded very high prices in the nursery trade. Subspecies *rockii* is a very hardy plant in cultivation; seedlings grow fast, but it takes more than five years to see their first bloom. See Figure 39.

P. suffruticosa subsp. rockii var. linyanshanii

(T. Hong & G. L. Osti) J. J. Halda in Acta Musei Richnoviensis 4 (2): 30 (1997).

P. *rockii* subsp. *linyanshanii* T. Hong & G. L. Osti in Bulletin of Botanical Research 14 (3): 237 (1994).

EPITHET: *linyanshanii*, "from Linyan Shan."

DESCRIPTION: Differs from var. *rockii* in having folioles lanceolate or narrowly ovate, entire. Flowering April to May.

DISTRIBUTION: China, in provinces of Gansu (Wenxian, Baimahegou) and Hubei (Baokan, Dashui), growing in coniferous forest, in thickets, and on rocky slopes at altitudes up to 1600 m (5280 ft.).

COMMENT: To my knowledge, this plant is not yet in cultivation. See Figure 39.

P. suffruticosa subsp. rockii var. yananensis

(T. Hong & M. R. Li) J. J. Halda, Acta Musei Richnoviensis 4 (2): 30 (1997).

P. *yananensis* T. Hong & M. R. Li in Bulletin of Botanical Research 12 (3): 226 (1992).

EPITHET: *yananensis*, "of Yanan," in Shanxi Province, China.

DESCRIPTION: Differs from variety *rockii* in having only a few leaflets (up to 11); petals smaller, sometimes purplish and reddish-purple stigma and disc. Flowering April to May.

DISTRIBUTION: China, in Shanxi (Yanan, Wanhua Mountains), growing in *Platycladus* forest.

COMMENT: To my knowledge, this peony is not yet in cultivation.

Discussion: The P. suffruticosa Complex

Paeonia suffruticosa represents a large complex of taxa or "types," the origin of which is often not very clear. They occupy a huge range in the Chinese provinces of Anhui, Gansu, Henan, Shanxi, Sichuan, and Yunnan. They are often found growing near monasteries, where they have long been cultivated for medicinal and ornamental purposes. Woody peonies have been cultivated in China for more than fifteen hundred years, and by the 1990s more than five hundred cultivars were recognized there (Hong et al. 1992).

In 536 C.E. the Chinese recognized two kinds of peonies: *sho-yo*, common peony, currently known as *Paeonia lactiflora*, and *mow-tan*, woody peony. The latter peony was called *hua wang*, the "king of flowers," and the former *hua seang*, the "king's prime minister." Both were grown primarily for medicinal purposes until about 600 C.E. Shortly after the Chinese began growing peonies for ornament, they established the Gow Yang Sew, a registry of cultivars, in which they recorded the parents, quality, and other important characteristics of all named varieties. About 724 C.E. the woody peony was introduced into Japan, where it was soon popular and widely grown, as it is still.

In 1656 the Dutch East India Company obtained special permission from the Chinese government to send a group to China. The group returned to the West with the first report of peonies (Smrz 1925, 47–48).

> In Suchua Province, near Chung-King, grows a special plant named *meutang*. This one is unusually protected and is named the king of flowers. It is similar to a European rose, but is much bigger, with prostrate leaves. Its beauty too is much greater than that of a rose, but it cannot compare in fragrance; it does not have spines and is mostly white or purple, but some are yellow or pink. This plant grows as a shrub and is carefully protected and planted in all gardens, cherished by aristocrats as their favorite plant.

In 1873, a missionary recounted in *Memoires des Chinois* that the *moutan* (*meutang*) was prized in China as tulips were in The Netherlands. The Chinese had by that time developed more than 250 kinds, including some with fragrance. The best forms were sent to the emperor to be grown in his gardens. Still, not until 1874 did the first two woody peony plants arrive in England, when Sir Joseph Banks who had read the 1656 report, asked merchants sailing to Canton to bring him some plants.

Lauener (1989) wrote,

> A cultivar with double white flowers, flushed with pink and with darker, rose-colored markings towards the base of the petals, was grown in the garden of the Duncan family near Arbroath until very recently. It is believed to be a direct descendant of one of the original introductions, and was moved to the Royal Botanic Garden Edinburgh in December 1988.

Western botanists speculated that the plant known as *Paeonia suffruticosa* var. *papaveracea* (now called *P. suffruticosa* 'Papaveracea') was the wild plant from which the cultivated forms had been selected, but no Westerner saw tree peonies in the wild until 1910, when William Purdom collected *P. suffruticosa* var. *spontanea* Rehder. Purdom made a second collection with Reginald Farrer in 1914. In 1925 Joseph Rock collected seeds of a tree peony growing in a monastery courtyard at Choni in southern Gansu. Stock from this introduction entered Western horticulture as the cultivar 'Rock's Variety' or 'Joseph Rock'. Although Rock wrote to Stern that he believed it to be a wild form, Stern (1946) did not separate 'Rock's Variety' from the typical species.

Stern included *Paeonia suffruticosa* var. *papaveracea* in the type variety of the species, maintaining only var. *spontanea* as distinct. This treatment was generally followed subsequently (e.g., Fang 1958). It remained unclear whether either var. *papaveracea* or 'Rock's Variety' could be considered identical with any wild form of *P. suffruticosa*. Haworth-Booth (1963) considered that Farrer's description of the plants he saw growing wild in Gansu tallied both with var. *papaveracea* and with the plants introduced by Rock.

Pan (1979) recognized three distinct varieties of *Paeonia suffruticosa*, two wild and one cultivated. Apart from the type variety, in which Pan included only *P. suffruticosa* cultivars, both var. *spontanea* and var. *papaveracea* were upheld. The latter was described as differing from the type variety in having bipinnate to tripinnate leaves, the leaflets entire or rarely unequally two- to four-lobed, and large white flowers with petals blotched deep purple at the base. The accompanying line drawing (Pan 1979, 43) shows a plant with leaves divided into 29 leaflets. The variety is said to grow wild in northern Sichuan, southern Gansu, and southern Shaanxi (Tai Bai Shan area), among thickets under woodland on mountain slopes, at 1100 to 2800 m (3630 to 9190 ft.) above sea level, and to be cultivated in Gansu and Qinghai (Haw and Lauener 1990).

Paeonia suffruticosa subsp. *atava* Bruehl was based on a specimen collected in the Chumbi area of southern Tibet (close to the borders with both Bhutan and Sikkim) in June 1884 by a local collector. A further specimen that appears to be very similar was collected in the Tibet-Bhutan border region in June 1906. The locality data for both specimens is vague and of uncertain reliability. Stern (1946) thought their provenance

to be dubious and believed that they might be seedlings from plants cultivated at lamaseries. This was no more than an assumption, however. Both specimens show clear differences from *P. suffruticosa* cultivars, being smaller in all their parts and having leaves divided into as many as 15 leaflets, the leaflets often cleft or rather bluntly toothed, usually with no more than three or four teeth per leaflet. The flower color of one collection (King, #549) is given as "reddish-white" and the petals appear to be entirely unblotched. There are also obvious differences from both subsp. *spontanea*, which never has leaves with more than nine leaflets, and subsp. *rockii*, which has much larger flowers with white petals blotched with deep purple at the base. Nevertheless, the floral disc entirely sheathes the carpels, which are hairy, so that this plant can certainly be placed within the *P. suffruticosa* complex. It is possible that these specimens represent a third wild subspecies, but until further specimens of more certain provenance are available its status remain doubtful.

The herbarium at Kew has a specimen from Bhutan (Gould 132) collected in May 1938 between Changna Na and Pharo (Paro) at 2360 to 2930 m (7740 to 9610 ft.). The specimen has leaves divided into about 19 or perhaps more leaflets and a solitary large flower with blotched petals and hairy carpels. Though it was originally identified as *Paeonia lutea* on the herbarium sheet (later altered), it is clearly a form of *P. suffruticosa*. Its collection locality is not very far from the general area in which the specimens described and named as subsp. *atava* (now identified as subsp. *rockii*) were collected, but it does not resemble those specimens very closely, differing most obviously in having a large flower with blotched petals. It appears to be closer to subsp. *rockii*, but the leaflets are quite frequently lobed, with up to five rather blunt, shallow lobes per leaflet. It possibly is an escapee from cultivation at a lamasery, and unless further evidence is forthcoming to prove otherwise is probably best considered as such (Haw and Lauener 1990).

Subsequently, several new specific names were published from wild collections (e.g., *Paeonia qiui* Pei & Hong, *P. ostii* Hong & Zhang, *P. jishanensis* Hong & Zhao, and *P. yananensis* Hong & Li), which I describe as subspecies or varieties. The whole *P. suffruticosa* complex is uniform in flower structure, a point that is significant for my classification.

Woody peonies were one of our special interests on our Chinese expeditions, and we saw many thousands of blooming plants of all wild species, except *Paeonia suffruticosa*, which can be seen mostly in lamastery gardens. We found wild populations of the last only five times, in Sichuan, Yunnan, and Gansu provinces; three of these were the "pink" type, close to subsp. *spontanea*, and two were typical of subsp. *rockii*.

22. *P. decomposita* Handel-Mazzetti, Acta Horti Gothoburg 13: 39 (1939).

P. szechuanica Fang, Acta Phytotaxonomica Sinica 7
  (4): 315 (1958).
EPITHET: *decomposita*, "of composites," here twice
compound, or bipinnate.

Key to the subspecies of *P. decomposita*
      Carpels nearly always five; leaflets and lobes
      narrow . . . . Subsp. *decomposita*
      Carpels mostly three or four; leaflets and
      lobes wider . . . . Subsp. *rotundiloba*

P. decomposita subsp. *decomposita*

DESCRIPTION: A shrub up to 2 m (6.5 ft.) tall; branches up to 5 mm in diameter, bark brownish or blackish-gray; small branches terete, greenish or purplish, with persistent scales at the base. Leaves chartaceous, 9–12 cm (3.5–4.75 in.) long, bipinnate or tripinnate, usually three or four, folioles ovate, obovate, or oblong-obovate, base cuneate, uppermost trilobate; lobes trilobulate, lobules acuminate; petiolules of terminal leaflets 5–7 mm long, of lateral ones 2–3 mm long; petioles 5–6 cm (2–2.4 in.) long. Flower solitary, 12–13 cm (4.75–5 in.) across. Bracts three to five, green, linear, 30–50 × 3 mm. Sepals three, sometimes four or five, yellowish, broadly obovate, 2.5 × 1.5 cm (1 × 0.6 in.), top abruptly acuminate. Petals 9–12, rose to purple, obovate, 3.5–4 × 4 cm (ca. 1.5 × 1.5 in.), top rotund, emarginate, base attenuate. Stamens numerous, anthers yellow, linear, 7–8 mm long, filaments white, linear, 5–15 mm long. Carpels four to six, purple, conic, glabrous, 12 mm long; style short, stigmas broadly recurvate; disc coriaceous, poculiform. Flowering April to May. $2n = 10$.

DISTRIBUTION: China, in northwestern Sichuan (Daduhe Valley), growing in thickets, on mountain slopes, in young secondary forests, and on riverbanks at altitudes from 2500 to 3100 m (8250 to 10,170 ft.). See Figure 40.

P. decomposita subsp. *rotundiloba* D. Y. Hong in Kew Bulletin 52 (4): 961 (1997).

EPITHET: *rotundiloba*, "rounded lobes," referring to the leaves.

DESCRIPTION: Differs from subsp. *decomposita* in having wider obtuse leaflets and lobes and generally 3(–4) carpels.

DISTRIBUTION: China, in northwestern Sichuan (Mingjiang Valley), growing in thickets, on rocks in sparse *Cupressus chengiana* forest, mountain slopes among *Quercus*, and on riverbanks at altitudes from 2000 to 3200 m (6,600 to 10,270 ft.).

COMMENT: *Paeonia decomposita* is a first-rate garden plant, recently introduced by us (Maerh Shan JJH9007, and the pictured plant, JJH920100036). We found several populations of this large species with more than two hundred adult plants, but the follicles were full of larvae and our "harvest" was only about fifty seeds. Slopes with this plant in full bloom are unforgettable: the large, silky, purple-rose flowers among the fernlike glaucous foliage look like something out of a fairy tale.

This species is distinct from *Paeonia suffruticosa* in that its disc covers only one-half to two-thirds of the carpels, while the staminodial disc of *P. suffruticosa* is vaginate. See Figure 40.

Section *Delavayanae*

Section *Delavayanae* (F. C. Stern) J. J. Halda, Acta Musei Richnoviensis 4 (2): 29 (1997).
Paeonia section *Moutan* subsection *Delavayanae*
  F. C. Stern in A Study of the Genus *Paeonia*, p. 1
  (1946).
Paeonia section *Flavonia* series *Lutea* Kemularia-
  Nathadze, Not. Syst. Geog. Inst. Bot. Tbiliss, Trudy
  Tbilisi Botanical Institute 21: 14 (1961), nom. inval.
Paeonia section *Paeon* series *Delavayanae* Kemularia-
  Nathadze, Not. Syst. Geog. Inst. Bot. Tbiliss, Trudy
  Tbilisi Botanical Institute 21: 14 (1961).
DESCRIPTION: Disc produced as conspicuous fleshy lobes around the base of carpels; lower leaves biternate, glabrous; leaflets pinnatipartite, with pinnae deeply lobed or toothed.

TYPE SPECIES: *P. delavayi* Franchet.

Figure 40. *Paeonia decomposita* leaves: (top) subsp. *decomposita*, (bottom) subsp. *rotundiloba*.

Paeonia decomposita subsp. *decomposita*

Paeonia delavayi

23. *P. delavayi* Franchet, Bulletin de la Société botanique de France 33: 382 (1886).

P. delavayi var. *atropurpurea* Schipczinski in Notulae systematicae ex herbario horti botanici petropoli-tanae 2: 47 (1921).

EPITHET: *delavayi*, after Jean Marie Delavay (1834–1895), French missionary and botanist, who collected for many years in northwestern Yunnan, sending more than 200,000 specimens to the Paris Museum, from which more than 1500 new species were described.

DESCRIPTION: A shrub up to 1.6 m (5.25 ft.) high, entirely glabrous. Leaves biternate, 20–27 cm (8–10.5 in.) long; petiole 7–10 cm (2.75–4 in.) long; terminal set of three leaflets carried well away from the lateral sets on a common petiolule about 6 cm (2.4 in.) long; common petiolule of lateral sets of leaflets 1–2 cm (0.4–0.75 in.) long; leaflets dark green above, glaucous beneath; terminal leaflet (of each set) thrice divided or tripartite, the central segment deeply and spread-ingly three-lobed with the lobes entire or toothed, the lateral segments entire or slightly toothed, oblong-elliptic, acuminate, mostly 5–7 × 1–2 cm (2–2.75 × 0.4–0.75 in.); lateral leaflets of terminal set deeply with four to five lobes, sometimes an additional segment (almost free) at the base, leaflets of lateral sets much smaller than the others, two- to four-lobed or -toothed. Flower about 9 cm (3.5 in.) across, with a conspicu-ous involucre of 8–12 foliaceous bracts set close against the five greenish sepals. Bracts persistent, ovate to lan-ceolate, tapering to the short- or long-acuminate apex, 2.5–6 × 1.5–2 cm (1–2.4 × 0.6–0.75 in.). Sepals per-sistent, suborbicular, thinly leathery, apex acute to rounded, 2–2.5 cm (0.75–1 in.) in diameter. Petals dark red, obovate, rounded, cuneate at base, 3–4 × 2–3 cm (1–1.5 × 0.75–1 in.). Stamens 13–20 mm long, fil-aments dark crimson, anthers yellow. Carpels three to five, each 1.5–2 cm (0.6–0.75 in.) long, glabrous, con-ical, flask-shaped, long attenuated to the small circi-nate stigma; disc produced as conspicuous fleshy lobes 3–5 mm high, around the base of the carpels. Follicles ca. 25–30 × 15 mm. Flowering April to June. $2n = 10$.

DISTRIBUTION: China, in Yunnan (Yulong Shan and Yungning areas), growing in open forest, on shrubby slopes, and among thickets at altitudes up to 2800 m (9190 ft.).

COMMENT: We collected this species many times. Different forms vary in the size and color of the flow-ers; probably our most attractive one is from Baishui (JJH90070317), with bright purple-red flowers. In wild populations, it is possible to see a range of forms from tiny maroon or brownish-purple flowers to much larger, bright purple to red ones. This species has been in cultivation since 1892; it is vigorous and long-lived in suitable conditions. Some forms are strongly sto-loniferous, spreading to create thickets of woody stems. See Figure 41.

24. *P. lutea* Delavay ex Franchet, Bulletin de la Société botanique de France 33: 382 (1886).

P. lutea var. *superba* Hort. ex Gardeners' Chronicle, ser. 3: 44 (1908).
P. delavayi var. *lutea* (Franchet) Finet & Gagnepain, Bulletin de la Société botanique de France 51: 524 (1904).
P. delavayi var. *lutea* f. *superba* Lemoine in Revue Hor-ticole, p. 14 (1906).
EPITHET: *lutea*, "yellow."

DESCRIPTION: A shrub up to 3 m (10 ft.) high, quite glabrous. Leaves biternate; petioles 8–14 cm (3–5.5 in.) long; terminal set of leaflets borne on a common petiolule 4–5 cm (1.5–2 in.) long, lateral sets of leaflets with common petiolule 2–2.5 cm (0.75–1 in.) long, rarely 3.5 cm (1.4 in.); leaflets incisely lobed and toothed but not greatly dissected, the lobes and teeth not much spreading, acute with the apex blunt, dark green above, glaucous beneath; terminal leaflet (of each set) about 10 cm (4 in.) long, deeply trisect, the middle segment about 3 cm (1 in.) wide and shortly three- to four-lobed, the lateral segments oblong-acute, entire or with one or two teeth near the apex, 12–17 mm wide; lateral leaflets of the terminal sets 8–9.5 × 3 cm (3–3.5 × 1 in.), shortly 3- to 5-lobed, those of lateral sets 4–8.5 × 1.5–2.7 cm (1.5–3 × 0.6–1 in.), 1- to 3-toothed to deeply segmented and three- to four-lobed or -toothed. Flower 5–7 cm (2–2.75 in.) across. Bracts and sepals together (five to eight), persistent, the outer three or four narrow-oblong to narrow-elliptic, acute, 20–70 × 3–8 mm, foliaceous; the intermediate ones oblate and caudate to suborbicular and cuspidate, about 20 × 15 mm; the inner suborbicular, shortly cus-pidate to rounded, 15–18 mm long, thinly leathery, greenish, often flushed with red and with a thin, whit-ish margin. Petals yellow (rarely with red spots), obo-vate from a cuneate base, rounded 2.5–3.5 × 2–2.5 cm (1–1.4 × 0.75–1 in.) somewhat concave. Stamens yel-low, 12–15 mm long. Carpels glabrous, conical, shortly attenuated to the very small flattened circular stigma, 10–14 mm long; disc produced as conspicu-

Figure 41. Leaves of *Paeonia delavayi* (top) and *P. lutea* (bottom).

Paeonia lutea, two color forms

ous fleshy lobes 3–4 cm (1–1.5 in.) high around the base of the carpels. Follicles 30 × 15 mm. Flowering April to June. 2n = 10.

DISTRIBUTION: China, in Yunnan and Sichuan, and in southeastern Tibet, growing on brushy slopes, among rocks, and in open spruce forest up to 4300 m (14,110 ft.).

COMMENT: This species was discovered by Delavay on Cang Shan in 1883; he sent seeds together with a dried specimen, and plants raised from these seeds flowered in France in 1889. *Paeonia lutea* differs from *P. delavayi* in the absence of the involucre below the calyx, in having only one to four foliaceous bracts, and in the yellow color of the corolla. Plants vary in size of stem and flowers. We collected this taxon many times: in Sichuan on Haba Shan just behind the bridge from Daju (JJH90060012); in Yunnan on Yulong Shan (Baishui JJH90080024); the larger plants illustrated on Cang Shan (Huadianba JJH840572); and the one whose flower, without red markings, is shown at the lower left of the plate, on Baima Shan (JJH840693). Plants from southeastern Tibet (Tsangpo JJH840715) are much bigger. *Paeonia lutea* has been in cultivation for at least 90 years and is an ancestor of many yellow and orange tree peony cultivars. It is easily grown in temperate gardens, where its huge seeds often produce volunteer seedlings. It is quite shade-tolerant, flowering well in a northern exposure with only two or three hours of sun a day. Plants may be damaged, dying back to the ground, by temperatures below about −15°C (5°F), but they usually resprout from the root.

Stern and Taylor described the Tibetan peony, *Paeonia lutea* var. *ludlowii* (also known as *P. ludlowii*), which is reputed to be much taller and have much larger flowers than the type; however, these plants seem to be a horticultural selection only. The species displays a great deal of variability. While plants in cultivation under this name are usually true from seed, it is believed that this is the result of long establishment in cultivation as a seed strain. See Figure 41.

25. *P. potaninii* Komarov in Notulae Syst. Herb. Horti Bot. Petrop. 2: 7 (1921).

P. delavayi var. *angustiloba* Rehder & Wilson in Sargent, Plantae Wilsonianae 1: 318 (1913).

EPITHET: *potaninii*, after Grigorij Nikolajevic Potanin (1835–1920), Russian botanist.

Key to the varieties of *P. potaninii*
> Plant growth spreading; leaflets deeply dissected; flowers maroon-red . . Var. *potaninii*
> Plant growth erect; leaflets shorter and more ovate; flowers yellow . . . . Var. *trollioides*

P. potaninii var. *potaninii*

DESCRIPTION: Shrub up to 1 m (3 ft.) tall, stoloniferous and quite glabrous. Leaves biternate, but the leaflets spreading and deeply dissected; petiolule of middle primary division mostly 5–9 cm (2–3.5 in.) long, petiolule of lateral primary divisions 1–4.5 cm (0.4–1.75 in.) long; petioles 11–15 cm (4.4–6 in.) long; primary divisions five to seven, pinnatipartite, the segments widely separated from one another and themselves pinnatipartite or lobed (the lower) or deeply pinnately lobed to entire (the upper), segments and lobes oblong, tapering to the acuminate apex, mostly 5–10 mm wide, up to 1.5–2 cm (0.6–0.75 in.) wide only in the lower part of the less dissected upper segments. Flowers 5–6 cm (2–2.4 in.) across. Bracts and sepals (forming a single series) 5–7; the outer two or three (rarely 4) oblong, acuminate, 25–70 × 5.5–6 mm, foliaceous; the remainder hemispherical to suborbicular and caudate or sharply cuspidate to rounded, 10–17 mm in diameter, the innermost two or three somewhat pale green, often flushed with red, strongly concave. Petals deep maroon-red, obovate to broadly obovate springing from a cuneate base, apex rounded or notched, margin slightly irregular, 25–30 × 15–22 mm. Stamens 13–15 mm long, filaments red, anthers yellow. Carpels two or three, glabrous, 12–13 mm long, conical-flask-shaped, attenuated to the circinate stigma; disc produced as conspicuous fleshy lobes, up to 2.5 mm high, round the base of the carpels. Follicles 15–30 mm long and very wide. Flowering April to June. 2n = 10.

DISTRIBUTION: China, in western Sichuan and Yunnan, growing in open woodland, on rocky slopes, and among thickets at altitudes up to 3400 m (11,160 ft.).

COMMENT: Of our many collections, the most ornamental are the illustrated red form from Minya Konka (JJH8406063) and a large white form from the northern Yulong Shan (Second Glacier JJH9008040). This albino seems to be the product of natural variation. *Paeonia potaninii* is a vigorous, fast grower that travels via stolons in suitable conditions and creates very ornamental clumps. See Figure 42.

Figure 42. *Paeonia potaninii* leaves: (top) var. *potaninii*, (bottom) var. *trollioides*.

Paeonia potaninii var. *potaninii*, two color forms

Paeonia potaninii var. *trollioides*

P. potaninii var. *trollioides* (Stapf ex F. C. Stern)
F. C. Stern in Journal of the Royal Horticultural
Society 68: 125 (1943).

P. trollioides Stapf ex F. C. Stern in Journal of the
   Royal Horticultural Society 56: 77 (1931).
P. forrestii trollioides Saunders in National Horticul-
   ture Magazine (Washington) 13: 220 (1934).
   EPITHET: *trollioides*, "having the form of *Trollius*," a
genus in the family Ranunculaceae with bright yellow,
globe-shaped flowers.
   DESCRIPTION: Differs from var. *potaninii* in being
more erect, with segments and lobes more oblong and
shortly acuminate; flowers yellow (sometimes white),
do not open widely, with large follicles. Flowering
April to June. $2n = 10$.
   DISTRIBUTION: China, in northwestern Yunnan
(Beima Shan) and Sichuan (Haba Shan), and in
southeastern Tibet (Tsekou), growing on open hills,
rocky slopes, and open spruce forest up to 3800 m
(12,470 ft.).
   COMMENT: Potanin collected this taxon in 1890 in
southern Sichuan, but his specimens were not realized
to be different from typical plants. Stapf described the
species based on plants collected by Forrest in the
Beima Shan. Variety *trollioides* is a delightful plant with
its erect, *Trollius*-like flowers, and it is a fast grower with
plenty of stolons. From our several collections, we have
illustrated a more robust form from the Beima Shan
(JJH8406137), and a smaller one with nearly closed,
smaller flowers from the Haba Shan (JJH90080014).
See Figure 42.

Natural Hybrids

A few natural hybrids among herbaceous peonies have
attracted some attention and been admired by gardeners. These are uncommon in nature and not especially
ornamental, but interesting to collectors. Chinese
woody peonies hybridize more readily, a fact that has
lead to the development of a great range of cultivated
tree peonies. The descriptions below deal with hybrids
that have been identified in the wild.

Herbaceous hybrids
   P. ×*majko*
   P. ×*chameleon*

Woody hybrids
   P. suffruticosa 'Papaveracea'

P. ×*franchetii*
P. ×*handel-mazzettii*

P. ×*majko* N. Ketzchoweli in Not. Syst. Geogr. Inst.
Bot. Tiflis 21: 17 (1959).

P. maleevii Kemularia-Nathadze, Not. Syst. Geog. Inst.
   Bot. Tbiliss, Trudy Tbilisi Botanical Institute 21: 36
   (1961), nom. inval.
   EPITHET: origin unknown. May be a person or
place name.
   DESCRIPTION: A naturally occurring hybrid between *Paeonia daurica* and *P. tenuifolia*, this has deep
red-purple flowers with dense tomentose carpels and
narrowly lanceolate leaflets. Flowering April to May.
$2n = 10$.
   DISTRIBUTION: Kartali, Georgia, growing on dry
slopes, in open oak woodland, and among sunny rocks
at altitudes of 300 to 1800 m (990 to 5940 ft.).
   COMMENT: This interesting, but not especially
attractive hybrid is sometimes found among plants of
Paeonia tenuifolia. We have collected about 10 plants
from several sites (JJH650911, JJH720895, JJH840713)
that are quite varied in the shape and size of their leaflets. Although of garden interest only to the collector,
they are very hardy, free-blooming plants.

P. ×*chamaeleon* Troitzky ex Grossheim, Flora
Kavkaza 2: 92 (1930).

   EPITHET: *chamaeleon*, "changeable."
   DESCRIPTION: A naturally occurring hybrid between *Paeonia daurica* and *P. mlokosewitschii*.
   DISTRIBUTION: Georgia, in Kachetia, growing on
rocky slopes and in open woods.
   COMMENT: This is an intermediate hybrid often
having bicolored petals. We found only one locality
for it in Kachetia (Ninigora JJH730634); there it is
infrequent, constituting about 0.05 percent of the
entire population and not very easy to find. Most of
the hybrid individuals have yellow flowers with red
stripes, or sometimes a few petals are pink or red. It is
a very unusual plant, unfortunately sterile and slow-
growing.

P. suffruticosa 'Papaveracea' in Bean, Trees and
Shrubs Hardy in the British Isles, ed. 8, 4: 81 (1976).

P. papaveracea Andrews, Botanist's Repository 7: 463
   (1807).

P. suffruticosa var. *papaveracea* (Andrews) Kemer, Hortus Sempervirens 5: t. 473 (1816).

EPITHET: *papaveracea*, "poppylike."

DESCRIPTION: Leaves with nine sharply pointed leaflets, terminal leaflet 3-lobed. Flowers single, petals white flushed pink, blotched with reddish-purple at the base, sheath enclosing carpels purple, filaments purple throughout their length.

COMMENT: This clone, known only as a garden plant, was introduced from an otherwise unidentified monastery garden in Guangzhou and was first grown in the West by Sir Abraham Hume at Wormley Bury in Hertfordshire in 1802. It is one of the most beautiful single-flowered cultivars. Similar to subsp. *rockii*.

P. ×franchetii J. J. Halda, Acta Musei Richnoviensis 4 (2): 31 (1997).

EPITHET: *franchetii*, after Adrien Rene Franchet (1814–1900), a French botanist who was knowledgeable but never visited China.

DESCRIPTION: A hybrid of *Paeonia lutea* and *P. potaninii*. A small shrublet up to 1 m (3 ft.) tall. Stems ca. 5–10 mm across, with lamellate glaucous brown bark. Leaves chartaceous, 12–18 cm (4.75–7 in.) long, biternate; leaflets lanceolate or oblong-lanceolate, base cuneate, dissect; petioles 12–16 cm (4.75–6.4 in.) long. Flowers 6–7 cm (2.4–2.75 in.) across; bracts five to seven, green; petals coppery orange, orbiculate, emarginate; stamens numerous, anthers yellow, linear. Carpels three or four, glabrous, greenish yellow, conic; style short, stigma broad, conic; disc lobulate. Follicles greenish, covered with persistent sepals and bracts. Flowering May to June. $2n = 10$.

DISTRIBUTION: China, in southwestern Sichuan (Haba Shan).

COMMENT: We found this hybrid in the Daju area just on the Yunnan-Sichuan border, behind the bridge across the Jinsha Jiang (?) River on shrubby hills and stony slopes. Plants grow among the parent species and are fertile. We have grown several seedlings, which are more or less uniform in habit and flower (JJH9006422).

P. ×handel-mazzettii J. J. Halda, Acta Musei Richnoviensis 4 (2): 31 (1997).

EPITHET: *handel-mazzettii*, after Heinrich Handel-Mazzetti (1882–1940), who was a noted Viennese botanist with extensive travel in China.

DESCRIPTION: A hybrid of *Paeonia delavayi* and *P. lutea*. A small shrublet up to 1.5 m (5 ft.) tall; branches slender, ca. 8 mm in diameter, with glaucous black lamellate bark; branches terete, greenish, with persistent scalelike bracts at the base of new growth. Leaves alternate, chartaceous, 14–20 cm (5.5–8 in.) long, biternate; leaflets lanceolate or oblong-lanceolate, cuneate at the base; petioles 15–20 cm (6–8 in.) long. Flowers 8–9 cm (3–3.5 in.) across; bracts five or six, green; petals coppery orange, obovate, crenate-marginate. Stamens numerous, anthers yellow, linear; filaments white. Carpels three or four, yellowish green, conic, glabrous; style short, stigma broad, recurved; disc lobulate. Follicles greenish, covered with persistent bracts and sepals. Flowering May to June. $2n = 10$.

DISTRIBUTION: China, in northwestern Yunnan (Haba Shan), growing on southern shrubby slopes at altitudes to 3400 m (11,160 ft.).

COMMENT: This was found above the village of Daju, growing rarely among the parent species (JJH9006315). The hybrids are very ornamental plants, on their native slopes appearing much more attractive than their parent species. In culture, they have proved uniform in color and shape of flowers. This hybrid is uncommon in cultivation but grows and flowers well. The uncommon flower color should assure a popular future for this plant.

Paeonia ×handel-mazzettii

PART II

Growing Peony Species

James W. Waddick and Josef J. Halda

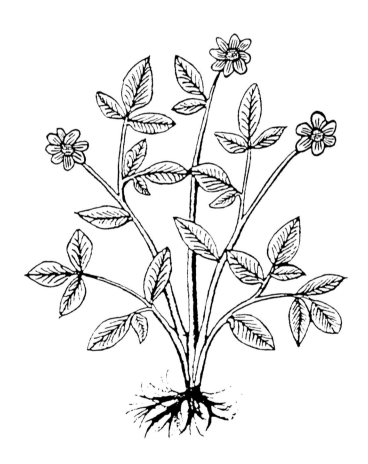

Figure 43. *Paeonia mascula* in *Livre des Simples Medecines, Codex Bruxellensis IV* (Opsomer et al. 1984).

CHAPTER 6

Cultivation

Wildflowers attract people for many reasons. Capturing these often delicate beauties can lure gardeners and growers in various directions. Some choose to tame these by selection, hybridizing and adapting them to conventional garden conditions. Others prefer to enjoy the true characters of the natural species and bend their own cultivation and climate to the challenge of accommodating the plant. The species naturally adapted to many temperate climates grow happily with little extra care. These have been grown for centuries. Some other wild species are more demanding and require specific needs to grow, flourish, flower, and increase.

The wild peony species are, of course, the source of all cultivated peonies whether grown as plants collected in the wild, or as selected forms and hybrids involving multiple species contributions. Most gardeners are very familiar with the hybrid peonies and the garden selections. Peonies are a main garden plant in most temperate gardens. The large, mostly full or double-flowered, herbaceous peonies have been the core of an international cut-flower business. In general these are very accommodating and respond to a variety of garden conditions. Ease of growth is a major consideration for these generally large-flowered spring-flowering perennials. These "basic" cut-flower peonies come mainly in shades of red, pink, or white and are grown everywhere peonies can be grown. Gardeners who have ventured into the various newer hybrids realize that these hybrids offer an extended range of flower colors, a variety of sizes, forms, foliage, and ease of growth. Growing the species reflects a return to the basics and wider interests.

Peony species have a wide range of variation—size and form of the plant, stems and foliage, growth characteristics, size and color of flowers, and more. The easy and distinct species are certainly the most commonly cultivated such as *Paeonia lactiflora* and *P. officinalis*. Other species are harder to grow and less common in the wild. They are more difficult to obtain and have cultural requirements that are harder to meet. Among these is *P. clusii*.

Wild plants can fit into a wide range of garden situations when used as an elite ground cover, in the perennial bed, as shrubs or small trees and some in sun or shade. In the following sections, I'll endeavor to suggest that by understanding a plant's origin, the gardener will have a better understanding and increased ability to cultivate the species in their own garden conditions. Unique needs of cultivation, propagation, and ecology can set the stage for a satisfying quest to bring these special plants into gardens.

Tree Peonies. I have avoided the term "tree peony" when discussing the woody peony species (section *Moutan*). These species vary in height from 30 to more than 300 cm (12–120 in.) tall. The cultivated varieties and selections have, to a major extent, been selected to grow in a middle range from 1 to 2 m (3 to 6.5 ft.) tall. In any other group of plants these might be considered low or medium-sized shrubs. Although none approach tree sizes, they are commonly, but mostly illogically called tree peonies. My use of the term "woody peony" does reflect a more exact and distinguishing character. Woody peonies have woody long-lived stems and are clearly medium or small shrubs.

Ecology

Peonies are nearly always described as temperate plants, suggesting that they may only be grown in middle latitudes. A significant number of peony species are found in very mild, dry climates that approach tropical latitudes and tolerate little or no prolonged frost. Likewise at least one species (*Paeonia anomala*) has a distribution that approaches the Arctic Circle and is extremely cold tolerant. Each species is adapted to its own singular state of environmental needs and conditions. Knowledge of only one peony species may not relate to others. Following are various general environmental conditions and some suggestions. Information that is more specific may be found under each species listing in chapter 9.

Soils

Peonies, in general, seem to have few special soil needs and thrive in rich soils with good drainage. Soil pH range preferences vary from slightly acid to slightly neutral, but with a decided preference for at least slightly alkaline conditions (a pH above 7.0). The woody peonies are found in more humusy, woodland conditions and will appreciate more organic matter in the soil. *Paeonia lutea*, *P. delavayi*, and their relatives can accumulate a layer of mixed dry leaves around their base and develop an organic mulch. These favor a slightly more acid soil.

Species from alkaline soils or limestone areas appreciate the addition of lime, but all species tolerate variation without a major dependency. Most herbaceous peonies prefer increased alkalinity, so the addition of lime is suggested in acidic soils.

The species may individually prefer a certain soil type, but in general they grow in a variety of soils from clay through sand and with various amounts of organic matter. In cultivation, they prefer good soils that allow good air content, do not compact, and have good fertility. Preparing the soil before planting may be the single most important action to succeed with more difficult species. Peonies are generally long-lived plants and can persist in gardens for decades without replanting. Experienced gardeners suggest digging a "$100 hole" for each peony as it will nurture your plant for a long time.

Fertilizing

The larger-growing species respond especially well to additional fertilizer, but all are heavy feeders and even the smallest species do best when the soil is amended with the proper fertilizer. If the planting soil has been properly prepared with compost, manure, and so forth, additional feeding may not be needed for a long time after planting.

Peonies respond like other plants that go dormant for long period and prefer a higher amount of potassium. While some growers apply a balanced fertilizer of 10–10–10 or 12–12–12, a formula with higher potassium and less nitrogen such as has been developed for bulbs can be even better in providing a good fertilizer boost. Commercial fertilizers such as 5–10–5 or 5–8–7 or even 10–30–20 all provide an extra amount of potassium. These products should be used according to manufacturers' suggestions and at proper application rates.

There is no large difference between granular and liquid fertilizers, although liquids will enter the soil faster; they are also faster to leach away. Organic and time-release fertilizers are longer lasting, but may release needed nutrients unevenly.

Any fertilizer should be applied away from the main crown and distributed around the dripline of the foliage to get good distribution. The timing of application is debated with some preference for fall application as the foliage is going dormant, while others prefer spring application as shoots emerge and still others suggest smaller applications in both seasons. Most gardeners apply fertilizer when time permits during the growing season. Care should be taken to not overfertilize at any time and small, frequent applications are probably better in the end than a single large dose each year.

Drainage

Perhaps more important than the physical and chemical make-up of the soil is its drainage. Peonies demand excellent drainage and none will thrive in overly moist or waterlogged conditions. A few can tolerate wet soils for short periods, but these wet areas should be avoided. It is always safer to try for increased drainage by adding particulate matter to the bed and breaking up denser water-retaining soils. There is a range of tolerance, with species such as *Paeonia anomala*, *P. lactiflora*, *P. mlokosewitschii*, *P. veitchii*, and *P. wittmanniana* growing well even in heavy clay soils, while the Mediterranean species prefer much sharper drainage and *P. brownii* can be found growing in screelike situations. Species such as *P. brownii*, *P. corsica*, *P. coriacea*, and others which are summer dormant will suffer if exposed to excessive rains except just prior to their active growing season. These should be protected and covered.

Planting peonies in raised beds allows easy control of drainage, while organic amendments to the soil can alter water retention. Peonies that go dormant quickly in places with intense summer heat and low rainfall do best in soils that seal over and provide a moist cocoon beneath the surface.

During their main growing season, almost all peonies do best with good water supply and do not like dryness during this time.

Exposure

Although peonies are sun-loving plants and require at least very bright situations in the garden, most are found naturally in open woodland, near shrubs or protected sites. Some species such as *Paeonia obovata* var. *japonica* and *P. obovata* var. *obovata* are touted for their preference for shadier sites. These grow at the edge of forests or in openings where full sun may be fleeting, but in cooler climates, mature plants do flower best when grown in full sun. The young plants of most species, however, may suffer burning if exposed to full sun; in nature, these young specimens would be shaded by surrounding shrubs or herbaceous growth of grasses, and their own parent plants.

Many tree peony species are found in woodland sites where they may have only brief exposure to full sun, but no peony thrives in deep shade. In cultivation, they often retain their large delicate flowers longer in sites protected from harsh sunshine. Even Mediterranean species may grow best in seasonal streambeds or deep gorges where they are protected from the surrounding very hot, dry climates and grow happily. Species from higher elevations thrive in moist climates with cool summers.

Generalizations are open to contradiction, but most peonies, when grown in some shade, have longer lasting flowers and show fewer signs of sun and heat stress. In milder climates, the sun's intensity and heat may demand that peonies be grown in even more shade and protection. They may also demand more frequent watering.

Hardiness

Peony resistance to cold, even requirements for cold, has been based on the widespread cultivation of relatively few herbaceous selections and cultivars. The wide distribution of species in nature makes it obvious that some species are found in nearly frost-free climates and refutes the general claim for cold tolerance in all peonies.

Much has been said about the inability to grow peonies in warm climates, but this does not follow when looking at all the species (around a 4th of which originate in the mild climate of the Mediterranean area). Other peony species are found in areas with mild winters and hot dry summers affording many possibilities to gardeners in mild climates. Unfortunately, there has been little development of hybrids or selections suited to milder climates.

As in other cases, a species' hardiness is best gauged by knowledge of the climate in its country of origin and the extent of its widest natural distribution. For example, a species such as *Paeonia coriacea* found in North Africa and confined to milder adjacent areas will be far less hardy than *P. obovata* native to the northern extremes of northeast China. Let common sense prevail.

The potential for developing a new race of mild-climate peony cultivars is great and has barely been touched. I'd suggest a plan of collecting and observing various mild-climate species in a mild part of the Earth such as southern California, milder areas of Australia, or along the shores of the Mediterranean Sea. Species that might offer some advances include *Paeonia broteroi, P. clusii, P. coriacea, P. corsica, P. emodi, P. rhodia,* and some forms of *P. mascula.* Many of these species grow and bloom rapidly from seed, and thus are good materials for commercial nursery propagation in mild areas. The American *P. brownii* and its subsp. *californica* have some potential for passing along drought tolerance and foliage, but their flowers are among the least attractive in the genus. Using this gene pool, with a wealth of flower color, foliage, plant size, and ease of growth, I believe new mild-climate cultivars could challenge the traditional more northern cultivars and extend the use and interest in peonies to a far wider geographic area.

Changing to the opposite extreme, peonies are well known for their cold hardiness. Cultivars can be grown with ease well into Canada, Alaska, northern Europe, and Asia. These colder adapted cultivars are relatively little affected by late frosts. In cold areas, new shoots are slow to emerge in spring and thus avoid cold temperatures that might kill new buds. Emerging foliage is usually able to avoid damage even with late hard frosts (−4°C or 25°F).

Even woody peonies with visible flower buds and foliage are able to emerge from seemingly dangerous frosts. Soft stems will droop precariously after a frost, but slowly straighten up with morning warmth. Frost damage can, of course, occur and depends on many variables such as the timing of frosts compared to the extent of new growth, the degree of frost and conditions of air moisture, snow cover, length of frost, and so on.

The ability to tolerate cold temperatures is not really very well known for less commonly grown species. Experimentation using common sense and good drainage may prove "the books" wrong about your own ability to grow certain "tender" species in your own climate.

CHAPTER 7

Propagation

Except for simple vegetative divisions, peonies present a few propagation demands in handling of seeds, grafting, and other methods. The following suggestions for propagation are generalities and may not apply equally to all species or even groups of species. Understanding exactly what kind of peony (woody or herbaceous) you have at hand will guide your actions. Each method of propagation will be discussed with some specifics, but experience will be your best guide.

Division

By far, division of mature plants is the most common and popular method of propagating herbaceous species. Generally, the home gardener will succeed best with division of an existing plant dug from the garden. The division process is most successful if done when the plant is truly dormant. Dormancy will vary somewhat from one climate and one species to another. Professional growers may divide and replant peonies at other times of the year with special care, but home gardeners will often fail to succeed if division is attempted at other seasons.

Determining dormancy is not difficult. This follows the extended active growing season after seed has ripened and precedes the onset of the seasonal change to cool weather. Dormancy may include leaf drop, drying and browning of leaves and stems. This also depends on the species, but in north temperate climates most species can be targeted for division in late summer through autumn or the months of September and October. Close observation and experience may extend this period a month or more in either direction based on individual climates, care, and the needs of each species. Species that go dormant early, such as *Paeonia brownii* and some Mediterranean peonies, can be dug and divided in midsummer. Immediate replanting will allow for good root growth before cool weather.

All woody and herbaceous peonies may be propagated by division of the plants. The best way to divide a peony is to dig the entire plant when it is dormant usually in late summer or fall and examine the root system. Herbaceous species will usually show prominent, often pink "eyes" on the crowns and base of the current year's growth. Using a sharp knife, hand pruner, or shears (depending on the size of the plant), the crown of the plant can be divided into a number of new propagules. Each new propagule should consist of a few of these new dormant eyes (or buds) and a couple of large storage roots providing for next year's growth. There is some debate over whether a small or large division will provide a better plant in the end. Those species producing stoloniferous growth are more easily separated into distinct new propagules for separation.

The propagules should be handled carefully to avoid damage. Some species may be quite crisp so that damage to roots or buds is difficult to avoid. Most home gardeners will replant the divisions immediately so no preparation is needed. If you plan on keeping a propagule for some time or mailing it to a friend, the thick storage roots should be cut back to 12–15 cm (5–6 in.) each, but this should be avoided if cutting will disfigure or damage the entire root system especially on smaller species which should be kept fairly intact. Top growth may be cut to within 2.5 cm (1 in.) of the buds.

Woody peonies need to be examined more carefully to insure that each potential division has good roots, good buds or eyes, and a vigorous stem or two of current season growth. Ideal divisions have all in moderation. Large divisions may need to be cut back to provide a balance between top growth and root growth. Some woody species form very tight clumps of stems, while others are more open and easily divided. Old plants of woody peonies often have very hard and dense wood at their crown and require a sharp knife, a small hatchet or saw to separate into appropriate divisions. There is a special consideration when attempting to propagate a woody peony that has been grafted. Grafted plants may be especially compact and dense until they have produced new stems on the scion's growth.

Division of woody peonies is often a more serious and strenuous activity than dividing herbaceous peonies. Digging a large plant may require a sturdy shovel, garden fork, pick axe, and extra muscle power. Roots can extend for 1 m (ca. 1 yd.) or more around the circumference of an old established shrub. Once dug, the roots should be cleaned gently and the relationship between top growth and roots examined carefully. Care should be taken that cuts are kept clean. Initial divisions may be rough because of the difficulty in making cuts, but a follow-up inspection should clean these cuts and eliminate ragged wood or bark that may harbor disease.

Root Cuttings

A special form of propagation is the use of root cuttings. This trait has been noted in some species, but not all. The ability to produce new plants by adventitious growth also seems to be inherited as some hybrids show this trait. *Paeonia peregrina*, *P. tenuifolia*, *P. officinalis*, and others seem most often to produce new plants from root cuttings under a range of conditions. Other species, including *P. anomala* and *P. lactiflora*, are shy about producing new plants from cuttings except under optimum conditions. Most species have not been adequately observed to confirm this ability, but garden experimentation is certainly warranted.

Cuttings may be taken when a plant is dug or when cut root pieces are accidentally left in the ground to emerge later. Commercial growers noted this with some frequency. Root cuttings may be made at the time of division by removing 10- to 15-cm (4- to 6-in.) sections of healthy roots for this purpose. Roots should be dipped in a fungicide or a rooting hormone with fungicide as a component. Plant the roots horizontally at a shallow depth of 5 cm (less than 2 in.). They may be planted either back in the soil in a protected spot or in a large shallow pot. Many roots will produce growth the following spring and some will delay growth for a year, presumably concentrating on root growth. Late emerging shoots are sometimes preceded by the development of a large callus growth at any part of the root. Callus development may also be absent. Clearly more study is needed on this propagation method.

Propagation by root cutting is also known as propagation by adventitious buds. Because the incidence of adventitious bud production is not well known (and some commercial producers have been slow to expose this fact as a nursery "secret"), this is a propagation method open to trials in home gardens. A number of common hybrids are ready producers of adventitious buds from root cuttings, and field propagation is most common.

Grafting

Woody peony species may be propagated by grafting. Most tree peony cultivars are propagated by grafting. Although a bit more complicated than other methods of propagation, grafting is certainly a process that the home gardener can accomplish with some degree of success. Because the process is well discussed elsewhere, this is not the place to go into details. Grafting requires a few tools and supplies. I suggest the gardener wishing to try this method read the literature in detail and expect losses. Grafting success will improve with time and trials. Even the best grafters do not get near to 100 percent success. The species most likely to be propagated by grafting are *Paeonia suffruticosa* var. *rockii* and its relatives, rarely others. Grafted woody peonies are usually slower to spread, but have a few other special needs.

Grafted woody peonies can also be propagated by division, but this involves some understanding of the results of the grafting process. A grafted woody peony consists of two different parts: the above-ground scion of the desired species and a below-ground nurse root used to produce the graft. Provided the graft has been done correctly and the new scion planted properly, the scion plant will have produced its own roots. You can only determine the degree of graft success and state of the underground nurse root by direct observation. Dig the entire plant (in fall, when dormant) and determine that the scion has grown its own roots and produced multiple underground stems each with their own roots and buds or eyes. These are suitable for division as described above.

If the nurse herbaceous root is still alive, growing and attached, it may not be possible to make divisions. There is some debate over the need to remove the nurse root and how well some cultivars will succeed with the removal of the nurse root. Most people feel that the nurse root should be removed if the scion has established its own roots. Again, this is a rather specialized procedure discussed in the literature.

Grafted woody peonies are usually much slower to produce viable propagules compared to divisions of woody peonies growing on their own roots. You may be unable to divide a grafted plant in the first three or four years unless a plant is especially vigorous and has produced stems away from the main growth or crown.

It is important to determine whether the grafted peony has had sufficient time to spread and produce new stems away from the main stems. There is also a balance between the growth of the scion and the growth (or death) of the nurse root. In one extreme the nurse root may die before the scion has been able to produce its own roots. Alternately the nurse root may grow to such an extent that its girth can hinder the expansion of the scion's roots. In itself, this may cause no damage, but in times of stress the shallow scion roots may make the drought conditions more severe.

There is also some controversy among some growers involving the overall vigor of a plant after the nurse root has been removed. Some plants may suffer more than others or take a longer period to recover from removal of the nurse root. Experience will determine the best methods.

Seed

Without intending to be either stupid or offensive, I offer as the prime rule for growing peonies from seeds: *plant the seeds.* This may not be as obvious or as rude a statement as it seems. Peony seeds have various special dormancy requirements that seem to cause red flags to be thrown about and make even experienced gardens assume the worst. They respond to immediate urges and put seeds in the refrigerator to stratify the seeds. Calmness and common sense should prevail.

As should be expected in a genus as diverse as *Paeonia*, seed germination patterns vary. Let's start with the basic method that can be expected to produce the best results for the largest number of species. An understanding of the natural conditions for seed germination should make these actions obvious. Seeds will naturally ripen in late summer to fall, the exact time depending on species and climate. When ripe, seeds may be deep brown, black, or blue-black. As soon as the fruits with the seed pods (carpels) split, the seeds would normally fall to the ground. In cultivation, the seeds should be removed and planted immediately. Seeds in nature are given weeks or more than a month of mild weather with warm soil conditions. In general, peony seeds need this initial period of warm and somewhat damp conditions to initiate root development. Shoot development may take other conditions.

The easiest treatment is to sow freshly ripe seeds. Seeds need not even be completely dark colored or totally hard. They can show partially dark colors and be slightly soft to the touch. As long as the carpels have split, the seeds can be harvested. Fresh seed germinates quickly and provides the best results.

Seeds should be planted approximately 1–2.5 cm (0.5–1 in.) deep in good garden soil or a potting mix. Whether in a pot or in the ground, the seeds need to be kept warm and well watered, neither damp nor allowed to dry out totally. After a period under these conditions, and I'll suggest some specifics to follow, the seeds will produce a primary root or radicle: only after this emergence will the seed be able to further its germination and begin the second stage of germination when conditions are again appropriate.

The second part of the germination process requires a period of cooler weather for the actual bud (embryo) to mature. In nature this is the winter chill. After the root has grown and the bud has developed and matured, the return of warm weather will allow a visible sign of germination with the appearance of the first leaf of the new shoot. The cotyledons, in most species, will remain below the surface of the soil and within the hard seed coat. Most species shown no sign of above-ground cotyledons. Technically this is called hypogeal germination.

The exceptions to this process include the following species: *Paeonia brownii* (and perhaps including *P. brownii* subsp. *californica*) and *P. tenuifolia*. Both produce long, strap-shaped cotyledons before the first true leaves appear. This germination pattern is common to many plants and is termed epigeal germination.

The best and simplest germination is achieved by planting freshly harvested seed as quickly as possible and allowing autumn warmth and ample water to provide the first set of conditions for root production. The temperate climate winter will follow with cold to provide the next set of conditions, and warmer spring temperatures will finish the sequence and work their magic to produce a seedling in the natural order of things.

Given this natural germination process, freshly planted seed, well watered in the early fall, will germinate the following spring—about six months later. If planting is delayed or there is not a long enough period of warm and moist, the radicle will not be produced, the shoot cannot fully develop, and visible germination will be delayed a year or more for the required sequence of events to me filled. Dry seeds or late ripening seed may take an extended period of warm moist before the radicle is developed, but once developed it can stay "on hold" waiting for the cool period needed for bud development, maturity, and growth. Any delay in planting fresh seed can delay germination. Germination may not be completed until the end of a second cool period followed by warmth.

Some evidence points to the development of germination inhibitors because of extended storage, resulting in even longer delays in germination for these inhibitor chemicals to be released. Peony seed generally can be safely stored for a number of years with little reduction in germination rate. Storage may result in a much extended germination period. Seeds planted in the ground, especially if planted in spring, may take a year or more to overcome germination delays, rehydrate, and complete the total germination stages.

Peonies have produced a string of variables. *Paeonia brownii* subsp. *californica*, for example, may not get enough natural rainfall during the warm days of autumn to provide the warm moist conditions described and its seeds will germinate when simply exposed to the cool moist conditions provided by southern California's winter rains. Both American subspecies will apparently germinate if ripe seeds are planted and kept cool (above freezing) and ideally around 5°C (41°F) for about three months or longer.

Woody peony species, especially those from milder climates, may germinate after a short period of warm moist with little or no chill required. These seeds when given warm moist conditions may produce a root in a couple of weeks and then produce a shoot just a few weeks further. The entire germination period to produce the first seedling leaf may be less than a month, which is against the preconception of an extended period for germination.

The variability described for the extremes of American species and mild-climate woody peony species relates in part to their native environments and knowledge of their natural conditions. Knowledge of natural conditions can be an excellent guide to anticipating specific germination patterns. Peony species native to climates that are more northern may be expected to tolerate or demand extended periods of cold for bud development. Mediterranean species may tolerate less cold and drier conditions. When specific germination information is not available, an understanding of the species' ecological conditions should be your guide.

This range of germination patterns has produced some old wives' tales about growing peonies from seed. Because of so many misconceptions, I have posed some comments or questions and commonsense answers. Let's discuss these and point out truths.

1. Is it true that dry peony seed will not germinate or germination rates will be very low; as little as one out of 100 seeds? This is simply not true, but does reflect that dried seeds develop some added germination delays and inhibitors that can only be broken by appropriate conditions in sequence. Dry seeds may need longer periods of warm-moist and/or cold and may actually require more complex patterns of warm-moist followed by cold followed by a repeat of these conditions to penetrate the hardened seed coat and remove any physical and chemical barriers. Germination may be delayed for two or three years, even longer. Germination rates will probably be reduced, but not so extremely.

2. *Is it true that peony seed should be stored in the refrigerator?* Although there are not good trials to understand storage in many species, refrigerated storage does *not* seem to help. Peony seed stored dry and at room temperatures will remain viable for years. Germination may be slower and more erratic, with lower germination rates the longer seeds are stored. Commercial seed companies and seed exchanges usually offer peony seed in midwinter. If planted in spring and well cared for, seeds can be expected to germinate the following spring, and may continue for another year or two.

3. *Is it true that peony seeds are tricky to germinate?* Well, yes and no. Peony seeds cannot be treated like annuals or simply cold stratified to germinate in a few weeks. Germination should normally be expected to take between one and six months, but can extend for two or three years or even longer. Understanding the principles and patterns of germination can produce good results more rapidly than most people realize. The beginning gardener is often very frustrated by the slowness and exactness of germination requirements.

Most commercial growers and gardeners propagate peony species from seed. The process does require some added understanding of the peony seed life cycle and patience. Pots of seeds or plots of ground need to be watched for years to complete germination of all seeds. They need to be weeded and seedlings move and replanted as they grow.

SPECIAL TREATMENTS. Peony seed can be manipulated in such a way that even seed received in midwinter from a seed company or seed exchange can germinate within the year. By understanding and manipulating the germination needs of peony seeds, you can have success even under less than perfect handling. Dried seed should be soaked in warm water until floating seeds sink. This may take a day or two or longer with daily changes of soaking water. Nicking or abrading seeds does not seem to help and can encourage the entry of fungus. After all (or most) seeds have sunk, place the seeds in a zip-seal plastic bag with a small amount of just damp moss or paper towels and place this in a *warm* spot between 21° and 27°C (70° and 80°F). Care must be taken that seeds do not get moldy, although a surface fungus usually is not harmful and can be treated by dipping the seeds in a 10-percent solution of household bleach or by applying a garden fungicide. Seeds should be watched closely and checked at least once a week. Seeds should produce a radicle in a matter of weeks or up to three months.

Naturally, there is variation among species and some growers suggest that differences in day-night temperatures are important, too. Success may be increased by placing seeds above a mild heat source such as a lamp that is on for at least 12 hours, then off for 12. Seeds receive the heat of the lamp for a period approximating a day-night schedule. Do not allow them to cool down too much in the off cycle or exceed 32°C (90°F) in the warm cycle. This variation in day-night temperatures may also encourage root production as the temperatures are gradually reduced to fall-winter temperatures, too. Imitating natural temperature cycles requires more involvement, but may prove ultimately more successful, too.

Once most seeds have produced a radicle of 2.5 cm (1 in.) or more, transfer the plastic bag to a cool spot in the refrigerator at approximately 4°C (40°F), but do NOT freeze the seeds. Seeds can stay unmonitored like this until the weather outside is frost-free. Plant these pretreated seeds in the ground or in nursery pots, allowing natural spring warmth to complete the process.

Once actual seedlings appear, I suggest planting them in a deep nursery pot 10 cm square (4 in. square) or larger with one to four seedlings. These seeds can be planted, root down, in single or community pots and stored cool as suggested above. Kept cool for three months or more, they will germinate on exposure to warmth.

When the germination of seeds obtained in late winter is manipulated in this way, the seeds may germinate in mid to late spring, but close enough to approximate a natural season. If held longer they may not germinate for an added year. Some care should be taken that seeds are timed to germinate as close to "natural" as possible. Seeds that germinate in midsummer may not have enough growing period to produce good storage roots to survive winters. Seeds germinating even later may have to be brought indoors, and it will be even more difficult to adjust them to natural climate cycles. Don't try to grow peony seedlings under light for six months and then plant them out in spring. It is better to time germination to the natural spring season.

A set of seedlings germinating in spring does best if planted in a special nursery bed where the plants can receive some extra care, watering, weeding, and regular fertilizing. Most peony seedlings grow under some protection from intense or full sun in nature. This may be taller parent plants or simply low-growing grasses, herbs, and so forth. Well-grown seedlings can bloom in as few as three years' growth whether a 25-cm (10-in.) *Paeonia tenuifolia* or a 1-m (3-ft.) *P. suffruticosa* subsp. *rockii*. First blooms may be few and untypical, only achieving normal size, number, and form in succeeding bloom seasons.

Growing peony species from seed may be the only way of obtaining plants of some rare species that are not commercially available as growing plants. You will also likely produce multiple seedlings, which can guarantee a good, if small, gene pool to assure better fertility in producing further seeds. Owing to the ease of hybridization, species should be given some distance apart to prevent unwanted crosses especially if you plan to distribute seeds as true to name.

Cuttings

Traditional cutting propagation appropriate for common perennials and annuals such as phlox, *Pelargonium* (geraniums), and roses is not possible for herbaceous peonies. Although this has been little studied and certainly not using a range of species, the stems of herbaceous peonies in general either totally lack nodal buds (which are the source of new shoots) or lack the primordial stem tissues to produce the adventitious roots of cuttings. New buds, shoots, and roots are produced from the specialized crown tissue, which may actually represent a modified rhizome, which is in turn a modified stem.

Woody peonies have potential for producing new plants from stem cuttings, but this has been little exploited. There are numerous reports of successful rooting of cuttings of *Paeonia suffruticosa* cultivars, but these require long rooting periods, specific environments (bottom heat, mist, and so forth), and plant-rooting hormones. Rooting is done from soft or semi-hardwood cuttings as for other woody plants, but success is often quite low. Plants are difficult to establish routinely and new rooted cuttings often fail to survive their first winter. The procedure requires very specific timing and handling and is best accomplished by commercial propagators, but in fact rooting most woody peony cuttings is so tricky that even professionals rarely have enough success to justify the use of cutting materials. Cultivars of tree peonies are more quickly and economically propagated by grafting.

Some woody species are stoloniferous (for example, *Paeonia delavayi* and *P. potaninii*) and these longer underground stems are more easily divided to produce a "pre-rooted" cutting for all intents. Certainly more experiments and trials with the species are needed to determine the practicality and ease of continuing these methods.

Layering

Traditionally this procedure involves bending a stem to soil level (or even slightly covered), nicking the stem below a node and protecting that node with moss, soil, or other materials to insure it is kept damp. Place a heavy stone or board over this length of stem. This should encourage dormant buds and roots to develop. Rooting hormone will speed things. After a suitable length of time from a few weeks to a year or more, the stem is cut and the new plants removed and replanted. This is an easy, simple method requiring little work for many shrubby plants.

Again a generality, but herbaceous peonies will not propagate from layering. They lack the required tissues to reliably produce new shoots and roots

Woody peonies are better candidates for this procedure, but also pose problems. Some have stiff upright stems that cannot be bent to the ground easily and these often are reluctant to produce buds able to produce a new shoot and roots. Successfully layered stems of woody peonies can take a year or more to complete; however, many Chinese cultivars are very suited to this procedure and are often propagated by layering the naturally produced stolons.

It is certainly worth the ease of layering to propagate a choice specimen for your own garden uses. Patience is required as some species are more inclined to root and put up new shoots, other not.

In summary, most herbaceous and woody peony species are grown routinely from seed. Since seed can be slow and somewhat irregular to germinate and grow, patience is of utmost importance. Seedlings may take three or more years to produce flowers and only then can you confirm their identification. Some specialty growers sell one- to three-year-old seedlings that can significantly cut down the wait. Divisions of species are infrequently available. Considering that most species, once established, are long lived and require little annual care, it is important to give young plants the extra care needed to insure success.

CHAPTER 8

Diseases and Pests

Peonies are remarkably free of most diseases and they have very few pests. If species are grown in accord with conditions similar to those in their natural environment, there are few problems. Problems arise when plants are growing in climates and under conditions that encourage specific diseases, most prominently botrytis.

Regardless of the following list of so-called problems, peonies are among the easiest and most problem-free garden plants. Gardeners who think that plants may suffer from one of the conditions described below should refer to specific books and recommendations to identify and cure these conditions. The suggestions given below are simply guidelines. Your own garden supply center or agricultural agent can give you current advice on dealing with the specific situation. These suggestions are not intended for specific treatment.

Diseases

Botrytis, specifically the fungi *Botrytis cinerea* and *B. paeoniae*, peony bud blight, can infect all tissues of the plant (although rare in roots) and is most frequently seen only in new spring growth. Symptoms are dark mushy spots on the stems or foliage that eventually dry and turn brown. Entire new stems may be consumed by the fungus infection and die. Rarely the entire plant is infected and all new growth or the entire plant may be lost.

The fungus is easy to control once recognized. Dormant spores (sclerotia) winter over in old stems and foliage, and start their active growth and infect new growth of the peony plant during the warm, wet spring season. The easiest control is through clean cultivation. Remove all old stems, foliage, and above-ground growth of herbaceous peonies in the fall and destroy or remove it from the garden. If composted, the sclerotia may still develop and produce wind-dispersed spores in spring that may continue to infect plants. Plants should be grown in warm, dry sites preferably with good airflow. Plants growing in shadier or low spots that have poor air circulation favor development of spore infections. Climates that have long cool, damp spring seasons may also favor increasingly severe botrytis infections. If new growth must be watered during early spring, it is best to water early in the day so that the ground and foliage can dry before cool, damp nights produce conditions that encourage botrytis development.

Controls are easy beyond the recommended clean cultivation. Plants may be sprayed with an appropriate fungicide at any season, but especially just as shoots emerge, but at least a day before any anticipated rain. Some authorities recommend multiple fungicide applications at shoot emergence, and twice more at intervals of 7–10 days. If the problem is severe, applications could continue as buds develop and any signs of infection appear and again in fall following clean-up of the season's above-ground growth. Spraying the soil at the base of the peony and surrounding ground may also be necessary, although some experts believe this is ineffective.

The classic treatment is the use of a sulfur-based fungicide such as bordeaux mix. This basic garden fungicide has been used effectively for many years. Most garden centers offer this fungicide as a premixed combination of copper sulfate and hydrated lime either in solution or as a soluble powder. Mix and apply according to manufacturer's directions and handle with care. Other more modern fungicides have proven effective, but read the label carefully to be certain that the produce has been tested and approved for use on peonies.

Other minor fungal diseases include *Cladosporium paeoniae* (red stem spot) and *Septoria paeoniae* (peony blotch). Both are comparable to botrytis in cause and effect and may be controlled as described above.

Pests

The most serious pest is the root-knot nematode (*Meloidogyne* sp.), a microscopic soil-dwelling worm. Symptoms are spindly pale shoots, few or no blooms, and lack of vigor. These symptoms may also appear from lack of good cultivation. Roots show signs that are more definitive. Small feeder roots will show gall-like lumps from barely perceptible bumps up to around 6 mm in diameter. Large storage roots may show increased diameter or evident large bumps. Small roots may also be curled and contorted.

Control is very difficult as the nematodes live in the soil and may inhabit alternate hosts for long periods. Some effective control has been noted by leaving the infected soil free of plants and bare for up to a year after removal of infected plants before replanting with disease-free plants. Commercial growers who can dip the roots before shipping have used various chemicals in control of the infected roots. These are generally not available for home use. Soil drenches may be useful, but these are limited and unproven. Recently adventurous gardeners have been experimenting with carnivorous nematodes. These minute predatory nematodes are purchased from specialty growers of beneficial insects. The nematodes are drenched into the soil where they seek out the root-knot nematodes and eat them. These beneficial nematodes have shown to be highly effective in some other ornamental plant uses, but use on peonies is still mostly anecdotal.

A common garden insect, the symphylan (*Scutigerella immaculata*), is an occasional peony pest. This very small, white, soft-bodied insect lives in the soil. Usually symptoms are difficult to observe as only severe infestations cause lack of vigor. The insects live in the top few inches of the soil and eat the tips of new root hairs, thus limiting the absorption of nutrients and water. If you suspect that symphylans are present, a soil sample crumbled on a dark background may show the pale tiny creatures. An agricultural testing agent can verify their presence.

These insects are more likely to be present in soils with high organic content, composts, and clay. They are often abundant in greenhouses. Control is effective by removing plants and leaving the soil bare for a year or by applying any measure certified as a control. Infestations are usually reduced naturally in fall as the insects burrow deeper in cold weather. They are rarely a major problem for the home gardener.

Cultural Problems

Other problems that may cause difficulties are related to site selection and cultivation. Avoid planting peonies in cold pockets in the garden where late spring frosts can damage new shoots, developing foliage and flower buds. Each species and selection will show some variability in its susceptibility to frost damage. Timing and severity of frosts will vary with the stage of development of the plant, so that plants that emerge early in a climate with late frosts can be severely damaged, while late emerging species subject to similar frost conditions may show no harm. Mediterranean species may be especially sensitive to late frosts.

Symptoms of frost damage may be a failure to bloom or severely reduced flower productions. Some buds may simply die on the stem. Leaves may be curled and crinkled or, in most severe cases, terminal parts of a stem may be dead. Peonies in general show considerable frost tolerance and shoots may be bent over 180 degrees from an overnight frost, but return to an upright position and bloom normally later in the season.

Care in planting is most important, but some protection may be needed, too. Cover the most susceptible tender young plants with a light woven or non-woven fabric on cold nights. Do not use plastic, which traps moisture and conducts cold directly to adjacent leaves. Some specialists construct lightweight portable boxes to cover very sensitive and rare plants. Experience with the needs and abilities of each species will improve your success in difficult areas.

Drainage and related water damage should also be considered. As mentioned, most peonies need very good drainage and prefer sites that are not waterlogged or do not remain wet. Heavy spring rains may form pools in and around plants for extended periods. Excess drainage from gutters and downspouts may unknowingly lead to delicate plants. Symptoms include a collapse of leaves, stems, or the whole plant. Heavy water soaking reduces the amount of air flow to roots and the plant can suffocate and die.

Correction of these conditions may be difficult if they are not detected early, and the plant may die. Divert water away from the crown of the plant. Move the plant in the fall, while dormant, or apply one of the products used for absorption of excess water (sold under various brand names including Turface). Conditions must be corrected or the plant will suffer and decline. Avoid sites that routinely hold excess water.

Ants

Let this be very clear, ants are not pests of peonies. They are mentioned only because beginning gardeners may be somewhat shocked when they find a sudden influx of small ants covering peony flower buds. The experts vary about exactly what the ants are doing, but clearly the developing buds produce a substance that is highly desirable to ants. Whether the ants interact in either a positive or negative way on the peony is unclear.

Some believe that ants eat sweet secretions produced by the bud and allow it to open fully — even that ants are required for flower buds to open fully. Clearly, this is not the case as peony buds will open without the presence of ants. Do ants bring any harm to developing peonies or flower buds? There seems to be no evidence that ants harm peonies.

Ants are an esthetic problem for those who wish to cut flowers for indoor uses. People do not like ants on their dining room table. The flowers may be shaken gently to remove the ants, or submerge the flowers and shake gently in a bucket of water to dislodge the ants from the flowers. Partially open flowers can be placed in a simple vase and left outdoors in the shade overnight for ants to find their own way back to their nest.

CHAPTER 9

Guide to Growing the Species

The specifics of cultivating the range of wild peony species are so varied that the earlier comments on soil, pH, drainage, and so on cover only generalities and far too poorly. Trial and error, experience, and individual horticultural abilities may conquer all specific needs. It is hoped that the following list of peony species presents details with comments on the overall ease of growth, the general cold resistance, and commercial availability. It is hoped that this guide will provide a few practical insights in growing the species. Some species are so difficult to obtain in any form that the average gardener should have some experience with other, easy species before even trying these rarities.

Obtaining seeds or plants of a new species, growing it to bloom, and establishing the plant in the garden can produce enormous satisfaction to the home gardener. It is hoped that these plants will be considered as special gems in the garden and treated as valuable specimens that should be nurtured, enjoyed, and shared by generous gardeners. Divisions and seeds should be shared with friends and they should be impressed with the very special nature of these wild treasures.

I have tried to use a few short cuts in species care. Each species is listed in the order of its classification and followed by comments on "Ease of Growth," "Hardiness" (meaning cold tolerance), and "Availability." By comparing these characters among and between species, the gardener will have a better understanding of the cultivation of a variety of species. As experience in growing "easy" peonies increases, confidence will increase and more difficult species can be tried. Many of these species are still unavailable or rare. The concerted efforts of a variety of growers will contribute knowledge and experience to wider availability.

Ease of Growth

Herbaceous garden hybrids and species selections (especially of *Paeonia lactiflora*) are probably the easiest peonies to grow and can be found in cold temperate regions around the world. Likewise, hybrid tree peonies are easier to grow than most woody species. Species listed as "easy" may prove more difficult in some climates, but individual care can overcome other difficulties.

EASY OR RELATIVELY TROUBLE FREE. These peonies can be grown in a variety of soils, sites, and climates. They also are widely grown and generally available from a variety of sources. Good species to start with.

EXPERIENCE REQUIRED. These require some special consideration whether of hardiness, watering, growth pattern, or something other. Growers should have some experience and success growing easier species before trying these.

DEMANDING OR CHALLENGING. These are not for the uninitiated except in or near the species' geographic origins. They may be difficult to transplant, tender, or characterized by specific cultural requirements. They require a good knowledge of the natural habitat and some experience growing related species.

Hardiness

Rather than give USDA hardiness zones, I have listed guidelines to climates these species may tolerate. It should be noted that most, but not all, peonies may withstand frosts especially during their dormant period. None are subtropical, but almost. Microclimatic conditions such as wind and sun exposure, moisture, and frost pockets may have significant impact on local conditions. Proper site selection may be essential.

Species listed as "Northern" will also grow well in milder areas, but those listed as "Mild" may not do as well in colder areas or may require more specific care. Do not expect those species that thrive in the most northern latitudes to thrive in the most southern and mild climates or vice versa.

NORTHERN. These species are able to grow at the highest latitude and coldest climates. All can withstand some exposure to temperatures below −18°C (0°F) during dormancy without significant damages. Most will benefit from winter snow cover, but may not require this added natural protection.

TEMPERATE. These include the wide range of species found in mid-northern latitudes where winter temperatures may dip well below freezing, summer temperatures may be hot and there may be some drought conditions. These have the widest tolerance to a variety of climates and may do well in warmer or colder climates.

MILD. These species will tolerate only light, occasional or even no frosts, especially when producing tender, new spring growth. They may tolerate lower temperatures while dormant. Summers in their native environments may be very hot and droughts common. Some of these species will not tolerate hard frosts after their foliage has emerged, but underground portions will come through similar frosty temperatures unharmed.

Availability

The garden hybrids and a few species are available in garden centers in all temperate countries. Most peony species in general are relatively less common and have fewer sources than most garden peonies. Peony species are generally available from more sources as seeds than as plants. Most commercial plants especially of less common species will be small, even one- or two-year seedlings. Large blooming-sized divisions are rarely available for most species. Here are the relative availability ratings for peony species. These are subject to change as more species become commercially available and propagation is more common.

COMMON. These species and selections are usually available from a variety of sources as seed, young plants, or blooming-sized divisions. Unfortunately, few species fit this category.

AVAILABLE. These species are available only from specialty sources, but may be purchased as seed, young plants, or less often as full-sized divisions. Most peony species fit into this group, but may still not be routinely available every year. Often only certain selections or named varieties of species may be commonly propagated.

UNCOMMON. These species are infrequently available except as seed from specialty sources and occasionally as young seedlings from specialty nurseries. This category is difficult to determine as individual collectors of seed may make certain formerly rare species suddenly available for short periods.

RARE. These species are rarely available except as seed or infrequently as young plants. A few subspecies and varieties may essentially not be in cultivation at all. Some rare species are not in cultivation.

Rarity in the classification presented in earlier chapters concerns the occurrence of peonies in cultivation only. Rarity in this context concerns their frequency in cultivation. Until recently, a few peonies were known from only a single or few plants in collections. With the recent introduction of materials from China (and elsewhere) some previously impossible-to-obtain species are now being grown and propagated from cultivated material. It is strongly recommend that inexperienced growers should not purchase wild collected material of any sort: seeds or plants. Because so many peony species are easily propagated, reliance on propagated materials should be of the highest priority.

Special Note on Availability: Buyer Beware

Peony species are wild plants native to their specific distributions on the globe. Some distributions are very compact, while others are widespread with large populations of many, many plants. Some sellers offer wild-collected materials whether seeds or plants. Although no peony species is considered endangered, some populations may be threatened locally, and wild collecting from these populations should be a concern to all gardeners. For others, cultivation is a means of conservation. If wild collection of seeds and plants is of concern to you or relates to the rarer species, please ask your supplier to verify its sources. Some suppliers are simply brokers or secondary sources and they may have to check with their sources for plant origins. This can be very "messy."

Nursery grown plants, even from wild-collected seeds will be more expensive than wild-collected materials. Be aware of this possibility and choose accordingly.

HYBRIDS. Peony species are well known for the ability, ease, and "willingness" to cross indiscriminately with other species in garden settings. Garden-grown seeds are very prone to producing hybrids. Special care must be taken to insure separation of species in the nursery. Hand pollination of species will increase the likeliness of pure-bred species, but insect pollinators are eager to alter expectations. Rare species should be grown in isolation to help insure against cross-pollination. Again, if you are concerned, ask the supplier how sure he or she is of the species identification.

Unfortunately there are misconceptions and misidentifications, and plants may "look like" true species, but are of unknown origin and may be misidentified. Some growers are just not familiar enough with the true species to apply the correct name. One of the most frequently misnamed peony species is *Paeonia tenuifolia* and it is one of the most distinctive species. I mention this because the common name for *P. tenuifolia* is fern-leaved peony. This common name is applied to a wide range of plants with finely divided leaves, often by those who have never seen the true *P. tenuifolia*. The name fern-leaved peony has been applied to various hybrids cultivars such as 'Smouthii', 'Early Scout', 'Laddie', and others. These named cultivars are all hybrids of *P. tenuifolia*. Although they all have cut-leaved foliage, it is always more coarsely divided than the true species. *Paeonia anomala* may also be marketed as the fern-leaved peony.

RARE SPECIES. In their eagerness to gain a new market, some sources of seeds and plants and growers of these may offer "rare" species by applying that name to an unknown plant. By assuming that a plant from near where a rare species grows IS that rare species, the seller has gained a premium price. Ask if the plant has been grown, flowered, and confirmed as the true species. Commoner species may inadvertently be substituted for rare species unknown to any of the sellers. Most species are impossible to identify as dormant plants or seeds. The distinctive red color and pungent odor of the roots of *Paeonia emodi* are an exception to this rule, but hybrids may share these distinctions.

Hundreds of scientific names have been applied to a much smaller list of true species. These names may apply to local distributions without distinction or be a significant variant worthy of cultivation. Species with a wide range may show some interesting variations that are garden worthy so let some of these "odd" names be a guide. The same identical peony may be sold under a variety of names without scientific or ornamental significance. Names listed as subspecies in this book may also be used on plants sold as true species by some sources simply because these names have been used in older reference books. Check the species synonyms in chapter 5 and the index for guidance.

Beware of exorbitant claims about the rarity and value of plants offered especially if the dealer is not well versed in peony species. Be doubtful of claims of identification until you have grown the plant, bloomed it, and checked it against descriptions such as those presented here.

Finally, unless you are the most demanding of collectors, there's hardly a "bad" peony species. Even a duplicate of a lovely plant you already grow is still a lovely plant. Each species has its own charm and all will show some special characters. Over time and as a specimen matures, you can see changes in size of the plant, number and size of the flowers, and a sequence of bloom. Understanding these variables comes only with the establishment of the "new" species plant in your own garden and comparing it to a variety of other different species. Experience and patience will pay off.

The species are listed below in the same order as the main taxonomic text. In almost all cases discussions refer just to the species, unless subspecies or varieties of a species warrant additional cultivation details. Plants with the same name from different sources may also show distinctive characters. I suggest that gardeners try using the keys and descriptions in the main text to confirm identification of plants. Very few or no cultivars will be discussed unless well-known selections are noteworthy.

Individual Species

1. *Paeonia officinalis* and its subspecies. This is the common native peony cultivated in European gardens for at least five hundred years. It was first used, then grown as a medicinal herb more than as an ornamental plant. The typical species is not especially common in cultivation, but many selections may be grown such as the double red (*P. officinalis* 'Rubra Plena'), double white (*P. officinalis* 'Alba Plena'), anemone-flowered (*P. officinalis* 'Anemoniflora'), and various others. The typical form is not as easy to obtain as the others. All make excellent easy garden plants.

As the four subspecies indicate, this peony is a variable plant and widespread in nature. *Paeonia officinalis* subsp. *banatica* is the least cultivated variety but is worth trying for its large pale-red flowers, while subsp. *villosa* is the most commonly found in gardens. Subspecies *humilis* is the smallest subspecies and well suited to any perennial garden bed.

Ease of growth: Easy. This is one of the first peonies known to European gardens, and wild forms can still be found on that continent. Numerous selections have been found and named, and a variety of hybrids exist. The species and its subspecies are well suited to beginning growers of peony species.

Hardiness: Northern to temperate. A wide distribution and lack of special growing needs make this plant widely adapted to a variety of colder climates.

Availability: Common to available, depending on subspecies and selections, but none rare or difficult to obtain. Subspecies *villosa* may be the most common and available as divisions, seeds, or small plants.

2. *P. peregrina*. This species has long been admired for the intense red of its flowers. In the garden, it is outstanding. It has contributed its genes to a number of modern hybrids while retaining a place of honor in the landscape.

This might be the choice for the person looking to obtain an easy-to-grow species that will add flash to the perennial border. Good drainage is essential. This peony is more often available as seed, but plants, especially named selections, can be obtained. The true species is somewhat stoloniferous so that over time the plant will spread out instead of forming a tight clump. This makes it easier to divide. The intense color has been contributed to many of the best red hybrids and makes this easy plant a good "exotic" for the beginner.

The flowers do not open widely, and selected cultivars show the variable color of the bright flowers. Selections in commerce include *Paeonia* 'Fire King' and also as "*P. lobata.*" This species propagates from adventitious buds on root cuttings.

Ease of growth: Easy and recommended. Good drainage and bright sun are important.

Hardiness: Northern to temperate. Widely adaptable and very garden worthy.

Availability: Available to uncommon. See source list. Fairly easy from seed and variable enough to produce interesting shades of difference in intensity of red color.

3. *P. parnassica*. The deep red to chocolate-colored flowers, short stature, and preference for good drainage make this a top candidate for the rock garden. This species is harder to find than some other species, but worth the search. Hardiness is not totally clear, but plants demand dryness in winter as wet and cold can be fatal as for many of the peonies found in the Mediterranean area. The species is found at altitudes above 1000 m (3300 ft.) in seasonally damp meadows.

The darkly exotic flower color and silvery foliage make this species unique although it was not always considered as distinct. Cultivation is similar to the former *Paeonia peregrina*, but more so; that is, better drainage and careful siting.

Ease of growth: Experienced. Not really a difficult species to grow, but does need some added protection and excellent drainage.

Hardiness: Temperate. Prefers a warmer climate and situation and does not do well in areas with damp or wet winter. Its narrow distributions suggest some demands and lack of wide adaptability. It has not been very widely grown so some trial is suggested.

Availability: Available to uncommon. The source list will provide names of commercial growers who can provide both seeds and young plants, but it is not a widely grown species. Expect to pay a premium price for plants that are not common in commerce.

4. P. clusii. This white-flowered species is well suited to the rock garden in a milder climate. Like many Mediterranean species it does not survive or last long in cold temperate climates. In milder areas it is easy and delightful. It grows to 30 cm (1 ft.) tall and requires good drainage. Many people consider this one of the finest peony species: a beauty.

This is also a good candidate for the alpine house where it experiences cool winters and controlled moisture. When well grown, it flowers well and is an excellent specimen. Summer wetness should be avoided.

Ease of growth: Easy to experienced. The ease of growth depends on your climate and some experience with Mediterranean species. If these few demands can be met, the species is highly desirable and worth pursuing.

Hardiness: Mild to temperate. Definitely not for colder regions. Although it will tolerate below freezing temperatures it must be kept on the dry side in winter. Cold and damp are to be avoided. There are reports of hardiness in northern regions if it is protected from summer rains and given a winter mulch.

Availability: Available to uncommon. Seeds and occasional young plants are in commerce, but it is not widely available.

5. P. rhodia. This is another Mediterranean species that demands good drainage and dry winters. *Paeonia rhodia* has clean bright-white flowers that are much admired. Another rock garden choice, but foliage is more coarse than that of *P. clusii*. Not often available except as seed. This is a very choice plant for a mild climate. Growing conditions as for its near relative *P. clusii*.

Ease of growth: Experienced. As for *Paeonia clusii* and similarly difficult to obtain, so experience and understanding are needed for success. Good drainage is important.

Hardiness: Mild. This Mediterranean species is able to tolerate some cold, but demands drier conditions. Careful protection can extend its ability to grow in cooler climates as for *Paeonia clusii*.

Availability: Uncommon. Expect to search some to find seeds. See source list and ask for this species.

6. P. mascula and its subspecies and varieties. This species is widespread and variable. Flowers are mostly red, but can range in various subspecies and varieties from pure white through pink to deep magenta. Height will also vary from 30 to 60 cm (12 to 24 in.). Some subspecies are very limited in the wild and poorly known in cultivation (such as subsp. *hellenica* var. *icarica* and the more recently described subsp. *bodurii*). Subspecies *arietina* and subsp. *russoi* are widely grown and admired for the richness of flower color and ease of growth. These are the forms to start with. If one were so inclined to specialize in one species of peony, it might be very interesting to collect all the variations within *Paeonia mascula*.

Growing covers almost the full range of possibilities, except for extremely northern climates.

Ease of growth: Easy to challenging. A couple of subspecies are easy and garden worthy, but others are uncommon and potentially more difficult to cultivate. Some confidence in growing ability is needed once you have managed to acquire one of the rare subspecies such as subsp. *bodurii*. Subspecies *mascula* and subsp. *arietina* are most common, but subsp. *russoi* is also around. Subspecies *hellenica* and var. *icarica* need good drainage.

Hardiness: Temperate to mild. Certainly it is easily grown in cooler climates, but some subspecies need warmth and protection so knowledge of subspecies distribution is required. Trials are needed to determine the northern growth range of this widely distributed and variable species.

Availability: Available to rare. Most of these are available in one form or another mainly as seeds, but subsp. *bodurii* and subsp. *hellenica* are definitely the least common. Subspecies *bodurii* was introduced into cultivation only recently.

7. *P. daurica* and its subspecies. This rather undistinguished plant has been listed as a subspecies of *Paeonia mascula* or given the name *P. triternata*. Although a good garden plant, its neutral-colored, pale red flowers and moderate size do not impress. It is however available and grows well, but does not have the pizzazz to recommend. A basic sort of peony more for the collector for the sake of completeness than for any special quality. Under some growing conditions the foliage may have undulated edges.

Ease of growth: Easy in the right climate. No special demands. Vigorous and long-lived in typical conditions of sun and good drainage.

Hardiness: Temperate. Grows in more open sites and widely adaptable.

Availability: Available to uncommon. Has been grown under the name *Paeonia triternata* and as such it may be more often available. *Paeonia daurica* subsp. *lagodechiana* is uncommon and may prefer a damper location.

8. *P. coriacea*. This is the only species native to Africa, even if from only a narrow strip of northernmost Africa (including the Atlas Mountains) and across the straits of Gibraltar to southern Spain. It is not commonly grown but is certainly a species to be sought for those in warmer climates. It may be one of the species that might form a new range of hybrids and cultivars for mild-climate gardeners. Little grown or known with little to distinguish itself except for leathery leaves (indicating a resistance to intense sun) and preference for a warm climate.

Ease of growth: Experienced. A native of warm, dry locations it demands both protection and excellent drainage. Plant in a hot site in full sun. Avoid extra moisture when dormant, especially summer rainfall.

Hardiness: Mild. Coming from North Africa it may be the most tender species. New growth emerges early and is prone to frost damage in colder climates.

Availability: Uncommon to rare. Only occasionally available as seed from collectors and specialty seed sources.

9. *P. corsica*. Widely grown and better known as *Paeonia cambessedesii*, this species is a favorite in milder and temperate climates. It tolerates little frost especially on new growth. In the right situation, it is easy, charming, and very choice. Because of its short stature it is recommended for the rock garden or front of the border. It has all the attributes of a very fine wildflower.

If your climate is appropriate, this is a recommended species and certainly a collector's plant in harder climates.

Ease of growth: Easy to experienced. This small species needs a warm site, some protection from summer rains and overall dampness, and excellent drainage. These conditions are easy in some climates, impossible in others, but the plant lends itself to growing in a large pot or an alpine house.

Hardiness: Mild to temperate. This extremely cute species is widely grown and commonly cultivated in mild areas such as much of Australia and Mediterranean climates elsewhere (including dry parts of the Pacific Coast of North America). Not suited for growing outdoors in mid-temperate or colder areas although there are reports of some success. It may be lost during some climatic extreme of cold or wet.

Availability: Available as both seeds and plants. Seeds germinate quickly and bloom may first appear after only two or three growing seasons.

10. *P. broteroi*. Although native to very mild climates on the Iberian Peninsula, this species is quite adaptable to cultivation and worth trying in cooler climates. It is able to tolerate more cold if care is taken that drainage is good. It is well known in cultivation.

Ease of Growth: Easy, but like many species from particularly mild climates requires good drainage.

Hardiness: Temperate to mild. This species does well when conditions are met, but if allowed to slip into weediness or damp soil, especially in winter, it can decline quickly. Certainly tolerates more cold than you might consider from its origin.

Availability: Available to uncommon, but irregularly in commerce. There seem to be few regular sources for this species. Sometimes found on a source list, it may be absent for long periods, too. Seeds are more common.

11. *P. anomala* and its subspecies. This species is surely more widely grown than might be determined from the literature as it is often mistaken for the common *Paeonia tenuifolia* because of its narrow leaflets. Plants may be sold as fern-leaved peony. When seen side by side with *P. tenuifolia*, the resemblance fades. As the only species near the Arctic Circle in its distribution, hardiness is not a problem. It grows in a variety of situations even along riverbanks so has some tolerance for dampness.

Ease of growth: Easy. It is among the easiest peonies to grow and is a good starter for new converts to species cultivation. Tolerates a wide range of conditions, including seasonal wet soils.

Hardiness: Northern to temperate. This is the northernmost species in the genus and has the greatest cold resistance. Surely it cannot get enough cold to respond well to growing in mild areas.

Availability: Common to available. Seeds are usually available, plants less often.

12. *P. veitchii* and its subspecies and varieties. This is a shorter species suitable to the perennial border without making too strong a statement. The charming flowers are a unique shade of raspberry magenta and the fine foliage is pleasing. Easy from seed and may bloom in a few years.

Ease of growth: Easy. A recommended species for its tolerance of many garden situations, including a damper site in spring. Does well in light shade or open woodland setting.

Hardiness: Temperate. Coming from a range of altitudes in central China, it adapts to cool temperate climates easily.

Availability: Available from many sources as seed and seedlings although less often as divisions or larger sizes. Subspecies *altaica* is far less common.

13. *P. obovata* and its subspecies and varieties. Often separated into two distinct species, *P. obovata* and *P. japonica*, both from Asia, are obviously closely related. Both forms have become more popular because of increased interest in shade gardening and the plants' ability to tolerate more shade than most other herbaceous species. They will not grow and bloom reliably in deep shade and neither tolerates drought well. These are among the most readily identified and distinct peony species.

Subspecies *obovata* is found and available in both white- and pink-flowered forms, while subsp. *japonica* is only available with white flowers. They are almost interchangeable in the garden except that subsp. *japonica* is smaller in all proportions.

Stern suggests that growing these in a west-facing site will keep them away from morning sun and generally allow a slow warm up and morning shade. Both may be grown from seed, and ripe carpels produce especially colorful displays of red and blue.

Ease of growth: Easy. Suited to woodland and shade gardens especially if sited where they receive a moderate amount of sun or very bright shade. They can tolerate some damp soil in spring and summer.

Hardiness: Temperate to northern. This species grows in northeastern China where it is exposed to temperatures well below −18°C (0°F). Subspecies *japonica* is more temperate and less tolerant of frost extremes.

Availability: Available. Until recently these would have been called uncommon, but the new availability from Asian nurseries has made plants and seeds far more available in the West. Newly imported plants require some extra care for them to settle down and grow naturally.

14. *P. mairei*. A Chinese species related to the above and benefiting from new imports. It is now becoming more commonly and freely available. It has not been widely grown or appreciated, and it has few extra points of interest. The flowers are various shades of rose to bright pink. This species is primarily for the collector, but it may have unseen secrets for hybridizers to try their hands. Probably treated as the above for all considerations.

Ease of growth: Easy and should be grown as the above. Tolerates some shade and damp soils.

Hardiness: Temperate, but probably slightly less tolerant of extremes than the closely related *Paeonia obovata* as it comes from central China.

Availability: Uncommon, but becoming seen from various new sources in the last few years. Imports are always divisions, and seeds are unusual. It is not widely grown so it is open to trials of all sorts.

15. *P. tenuifolia* and its subspecies. The fern-leaved peonies are among the most distinctive species that are readily available. The typical form has a simple, single deep-red flower, but is not nearly so widely available as the selection *Paeonia tenuifolia* 'Flore Pleno', which has multipetaled (double) darker red flowers. The double-red fern-leaved peony is highly recommended especially for northern and cool climate areas. It tends to go dormant early in summer and is therefore best sited where it can get some summer moisture. Most growers suggest a slightly shaded spot where it can get protection from the fiercest western sun. The fine foliage is readily subject to burn by the intense rays of the summer sun.

Less common than the double red form in order of rarity are the three singles: red, pink, and white (the typical species, and the cultivars 'Rosea' and 'Alba'). You may also see *Paeonia lithophila* listed as a dwarf form, but this variability in stature may be expected from a species with its wide distribution. *Paeonia tenuifolia* subsp. *biebersteiniana* differs primarily by its coarser foliage.

Ease of growth: Easy to experienced. Good drainage is needed, and the plant has a tendency to emerge early in spring when it can be subject to frost damage in some situations. Most growers suggest an alkaline soil with full sun, but in harsh climates, this will encourage early dormancy even as early as August.

Seeds are often available and easy to grow. It is one of the few species to produce above-ground cotyledons, and the first true leaves are not especially divided so it is doubly difficult to keep weed-free. More typical foliage appears in its second year and bloom can be expected in the 4th year.

There is some debate about whether *Paeonia tenuifolia* can produce adventitious buds, from root cuttings. This is a subject for an adventurous gardener in a climate well suited to growing this species.

Hardiness: Northern and temperate. It can tolerate quite cold climates if placed in more sun and given good soil conditions. It is also adaptable to warmer climates if given more shade.

Availability: Available as the double red selection, but all other single forms and subspecies are uncommon or rare. There is always a demand for the single forms and it is surprising that propagators have not met this demand with greater availability. 'Rosea' is occasionally available for a premium price, but 'Alba' is extremely uncommon. The species hybridizes readily to produce a wide range of single-flowered plants that are very easy to grow, have similar (although usually less finely cut) foliage and single red flowers. These may be sold as fern-leaved peonies, so let the buyer beware. These hybrids are deservedly popular and are fine additions to the perennial garden. They are generally more tolerant of cultural conditions and easier to grow than the species.

16. P. emodi and its subspecies. This is one of the true beauties of the genus and among the tallest herbaceous peonies. It is the parent of the hybrid *Paeonia* 'White Innocence', a Saunder's hybrid that can reach to 1.5 m (5 ft.). It is a Himalayan species that may prove hardy in a protected northern spot, but is far more satisfactory in warm-temperate climates where it is recommended. The typical form has distinctive red, odd smelling roots. It appreciates a shaded woodland spot.

Stern suggests growing this in a north-facing location so that its early shoots are less like to be damaged by frost and it will also have protection from cold spring winds.

Ease of growth: Easy to experienced, depending on climate. Good drainage and semi-woodland conditions seem best. Subspecies *sterniana*, a smaller version of subsp. *emodi*, is presumably similar, but almost unknown in cultivation.

Hardiness: Temperate or mild. Treated as a subtropical alpine, this species does fine where there are cooler summers, milder winters, snow cover, and moderation overall. Supposedly collections from higher elevation have greater hardiness, but perhaps trade this for less heat tolerance. Does less well in areas with hot summers, severe winters, and lack of snow cover such as the U.S. Midwest.

Availability: Available to rare. While the typical subsp. *emodi* may be obtained as seeds, seedlings, and divisions, subsp. *sterniana* is almost impossible to obtain.

17. P. mlokosewitschii. Some plants have a certain "something," a charisma, or mystique, call it what you will. This Caucasian beauty definitely has IT. In fact, this species has everything: it is popular, available, and easy to grow and has distinctive form, foliage, and clear yellow flowers, rare in the genus. The plant blooms early and has fleeting flowers, but charms all. The flower color in the best selections is a clear pale yellow; a range of colors from yellow to pink are found in the hybrids, which form easily.

The plant was named for the Polish plant collector and botanist, J. L. Mlokosewicz. There is a lot of discussion and disagreement over the correct spelling and pronunciation of his name. This species is widely known as "Molly-the-witch," a play on this confusion. Of course, the strict botanist hates this nickname and looks down on those who would stoop to use it, while others both amateur and professional use this name in only the kindest and most familiar sort of way.

Ease of growth: Easy to experienced. This species does well in a variety of sunny well-drained positions, but it also tolerates damp soils in spring and summer. In nature it apparently occurs in sites subject to some spring flooding. It may be among the most moisture tolerant species, but good drainage will still keep water from drowning the roots. It is a recommend garden plant and appreciates a damper site in alkaline soils.

Hardiness: Temperate. This species seems to be quite variable in tolerance to cold and can be properly sited in both warmer and colder climates and still perform well. Seed-grown plants may also be more variable in relation to hardiness. Because it has a wide tolerance range, it might be best to provide some protection in hot southern climates and more exposure in cool climates. During hot dry summers it tends to go dormant early and can look ratty. Extra moisture is appreciated.

Availability: Available from a variety of sources, but quality varies. If possible view the flowers first to make sure they are a good clean yellow or other preferred shade of color. Hybrids and seed-grown plants may exhibit a range of shades and tones including various yellows, pale pinks, and clear white. Most colors are clean, but may not be the clear bright yellow you might expect. There are a few named selections.

18. *P. wittmanniana* and its subspecies. Considered a "baby brother" to *Paeonia mlokosewitschii*, this species is very close to the above. This species may have pale yellow flowers, but cream or near-white flowers are more common. Again, while good drainage is always best, this species also tolerates soil dampness in the active growing season. The remarks for *P. mlokosewitschii* in general apply here as well. The bold foliage of both species are excellent garden features.

Ease of growth: Easy to experienced, exactly as described for *Paeonia mlokosewitschii*.

Hardiness: Temperate as for *Paeonia mlokosewitschii*. This too is a good garden plant for temperate gardens.

Availability: Available for both subspecies. Since both subspecies bloom early and fleetingly, the one thing that is in the favor of subsp. *macrophylla* is that it has such bold foliage with good substance that it looks better as a foliage plant for most of the growing season.

19. *P. lactiflora*. This is THE peony to most novice gardeners. It is also known as the Chinese peony (for its origin) or simply garden peony (as opposed to hybrids). For years it was also known as "*P. albiflora*" and was the white peony when it entered Europe in the 18th century. It has a wide distribution and natural variation from the pure "milk" white as the name suggests to a variety of pink to rose to near red colors. Numerous selections and named cultivars are available in all peony flower forms from single to full double and colors from white to deep reddish purple. This is the standard garden peony for most gardeners.

Although the typical wild forms are characterized by multiple flowers per stem, the named selections especially those used in the cut flower industry stress single- or few-flowered stems. Probably hundreds of peonies are simply selections of this species, not hybrids originating in Europe, North America, China, and elsewhere.

In addition to being a good species for beginners, this peony also can be used by itself, in its many forms and selections, to create an entire garden with no other species or hybrids needed.

Many selections are very eager bloomers and the backbone of the cut peony flower industry. Thousands of cut flowers find their way to markets in Europe, North America, Australia, and elsewhere.

Ease of growth: Easy to maybe even exceptionally easy. This species tolerates a variety of garden practices and abuse reflecting its natural occurrences in dry or damp locations. Extremely flexible, but does not tolerate as much shade as other peonies. Should be grown in full sun and retains good foliage until near frost.

Hardiness: Temperate and widely adaptable in situations. This is the work horse of the genus. Although it can be grown in northern cold and more temperate climates, it does not grow as well in milder climates, but selections may vary.

Availability: Common especially as selections. The typical single white species is probably among the least common forms. It can be grown from seed, and seedlings may be quite variable.

20. *P. brownii* and its subspecies. This is the only species native to North America. Although the species is generally considered confined to the Northwest, subsp. *californica* is distributed in Southern California and subsp. *brownii* is distributed east to Wyoming and Utah. Neither subspecies is a pretty garden ornament. The flowers are dull brownish and pendant, mostly hidden in the foliage. They are common in habitat, but rare in cultivation due to the cultural difficulties. They are generally collector's plants.

Subspecies *brownii* is perfectly hardy down to winter lows of −18°C (0°F), while subsp. *californica* does not tolerate much frost either in bloom or in foliage. The former does not produce foliage until early spring, while the latter has foliage that appears with the onset of fall rains into the cool of winter, although in colder climates, foliage will delay emergence until milder weather. Both are summer dormant and appreciate the summer baking called for many more bulbous plants.

Subspecies *brownii* has a wider distribution and a greater tolerance for growing conditions. It accepts various cultivation practices as long as drainage is excellent and there are no excessive summer rains or high humidity. Subspecies *californica*, with its smaller range, has more cultural conditions. It is essentially a near-desert succulent. The size of the plant and its distinctive foliage have some garden worthiness, and as a parent, this species might lead to hybrids suited to warm dry locations, certainly with more extreme Mediterranean climates. When dormant, it can appear desiccated and dead. It obtains almost no water in nature during its dormant period when it may go for a year or more with no rain. The shredded remains of old stems and bracts may help collect a limited amount of morning dew or infrequent fog to sustain it.

Ease of growth: Challenging, but plants respond well to a good understanding of their needs especially improved drainage, water, and cold tolerance. Both can only be recommended to collectors willing to work at growing these species. They may pose new and potentially interesting characters for the hybridizer, but their cultivation demands may be difficult to overcome. Both species resent too much dampness except in full growth and little summer moisture.

Hardiness: Temperate for subsp. *brownii*, but demanding of good drainage; it can endure temperatures to −18°C (0°F). Mild for subsp. *californica*, which is less tolerant of frost on its foliage.

Availability: Uncommon to rare. Seeds of both are available from a few specialty seed suppliers and occasionally in seed exchanges. Small plants and seedlings are even less common, and blooming-sized divisions nearly impossible to obtain. Patience is required for most species, but perhaps even more with these North American representatives.

21. *P. suffruticosa* and its subspecies and varieties. This woody peony along with its various cultivars and hybrids has been the basic tree peony in Western and Eastern gardens. Century-old selections and hybrids are highly prized. Wild plants occupy a variety of situations, but appreciate woodland conditions and light shade to perform at their best. In milder climates some forms can bloom extremely early in late winter or early spring. This and the next species have a slight preference for limestone, unlike the smaller woody peonies of the *Paeonia delavayi* group.

It should be noted that not all of these subspecies are equally easy to cultivate, hardy, or available, and they show a wide range in many characteristics, thus their frequent name changes and taxonomic reassignments. Hybrids, particularly with the closely related *Paeonia lutea*, have produced some astonishing colors in the cream, yellow, orange, and copper side of the spectrum. *Paeonia suffruticosa* subsp. *ostii* is widely grown in China as a medicinal herb and subsp. *rockii* is considered the king of peonies by many growers, thus running the gamut from "field crop" to "royalty" in the same range of subspecies.

Some names have changed from cultivar (*Paeonia suffruticosa* 'Rock's Variety') to species (*P. suffruticosa* subsp. *rockii*) and from species (*P. papaveracea*) to cultivar (*P. suffruticosa* 'Papaveracea'). Buyer beware.

Ease of growth: Easy with understanding of their special needs as woody shrubs, not herbaceous perennials. Above-ground woody stems are long lived and plants should not be cut to the ground when dormant. Some forms may be more sensitive to fungal diseases, so appropriate fungicide treatment should be kept at hand.

Hardiness: Temperate to tender with more leaning to temperate conditions. Given deep snow or artificial cover, some can be grown in cold climates. These species, subspecies, and selections as well as their hybrids are among the cold hardiest woody peonies.

Availability: Uncommon as species, but cultivars are common in local nurseries and garden centers. Specialty nurseries provide good selections of species, and seeds are sometimes available. New imports from China are allowing the true species better access to collector-gardeners.

22. *P. decomposita* and its subspecies. This species has only been known for a short time and half of that as *Paeonia szechuanica*; it is rare in cultivation. In nature it is found as an understory shrub to 1.8 m (6 ft.) or more in height. Those with experience suggest it is a first-rate garden plant and beautiful in flower with cut glaucous foliage and large purple-rose flowers. This species obviously deserves wider introduction into cultivation.

Ease of growth: Easy as for other woody peonies, but little experience in cultivation. May also be prone to fungal diseases. Woodland conditions.

Hardiness: Temperate as for *Paeonia suffruticosa*. Some protection is probably necessary in cold climates especially for new plantings.

Availability: Rare. Although found in a few collections, it has not been wide spread even as seed. As it proves its garden worthiness, more access is likely.

23. *P. delavayi.* This is one of the shorter woody peonies and some forms are highly stoloniferous so the overall form may be like a thicket of short stems. The flowers are generally smaller than most other woody peonies and carried deep in the foliage, but the bright colors are quite garden worthy. The names of this species and close relatives have been changed and switched often. This name is usually applied to red-flowered forms, but may range from unattractive dull brown to bright red or towards purple. Once established it is a long-lived and vigorous garden plant.

Recently some botanists have considered *Paeonia delavayi*, *P. lutea*, and *P. potaninii* to all belong to this species. Chinese botanists have proposed that these variants all blend in the wild. They all share cultivation practices.

Ease of growth: Easy in the right climate or once established. This grows in more open situations.

Hardiness: Temperate, but can adapt to southern ranges depending on origin of plants. Native to higher altitudes in southwestern China.

Availability: Available to uncommon depending on selections. Seeds are frequently available and may show a variety of colors and forms.

24. *P. lutea*. This woody peony is the yellow hallmark of the genus with 8-cm (3-in.) flowers of bright yellow. It is the main parent of all yellow, orange, and copper tree peony cultivars. In the wild it is fairly wide spread and plants vary in color, flower size, and plant size. The seeds are among the largest in the genus. *Paeonia ludlowii* is somewhat problematic, considered by some a mere horticultural variant of *P. lutea* and by others suited to species rank, a situation that will require additional field and laboratory research.

Ease of growth: Easy with the same warnings as other woody peonies. Newly acquired plants may take some time and care to settle down.

Hardiness: Temperate, but requiring some protection in colder areas. Does well in partial sun.

Availability: Available, but it is frequently seen as a form or subspecies named "Ludlowii," which is widely cultivated. Easily grown from seeds that are large even by peony standards.

25. *P. potaninii* and its varieties. Although this species has been cultivated for a long time, it has never been of major importance among peony growers. The variety of flower colors and their willingness to produce hybrids has been the basis for a number of name changes. Seedlings, depending on the source, may show a range of colors, including near white to yellow, orange, red, and near brown. Established plants are stoloniferous and form open dwarf shrubs.

Variety *trollioides* with finely cut foliage and cheery yellow single flowers is a wonderful garden plant in the right location. It makes an excellent addition to the perennial border. A white form is less common but equally winning.

Ease of growth: Easy to some experience required. As a forest and forest edge dwarf shrub, it does best in a loose woodland soil and with near constant or even moisture. Light shade but more sun in the right climate.

Hardiness: Temperate to tender. This is found in a milder part of China, but sometimes at a high altitude so hardiness will vary. Winter protection may be needed if you try to grow this in northern climates; heavy snow cover and constant low temperatures may also help.

Availability: Available both as seeds and plants. Due to its stoloniferous growth, divisions are easy. Plants tend to be prolific seeders in the right location. Sources may list varieties by color and your preferences should guide you.

Peony Species for Beginning Growers

Often the beginner in any area wants a hint of how to start and what plants to obtain to assure some success and more encouragement to continue. An informal survey was conducted of peony growers in North America, Australia, and Europe and it consisted of the question "What are the five best species for your location?" The answers were surprisingly consistent in suggesting species that are valued for their flowers, foliage, and garden value as well as those which are more commonly available in commerce.

NORTH AMERICA. The majority of the North American responses were from northern climates including Canada and Alaska. These are the traditional areas for growing the numerous selections, hybrids, and cultivars of *Paeonia lactiflora* and *P. officinalis. Paeonia tenuifolia*, the fern-leaved peony, occurred on almost every list. Although most growers signified the typically available double, red-flowered form, mention was also made of the single red- and single pink-flowered forms. This is perhaps the most unique and readily identifiable species in the genus. Obviously this species is widely adaptable and very satisfactory.

The rest of the list was more variable, but the next most commonly grown species were *Paeonia mlokosewitschii* and *P. veitchii*. These are also among the more distinct species. The former has distinctive, single large pale-yellow flowers and bold foliage, while the later is a charming dwarf species with bright raspberry-pink flowers. Both are available as seed, easily germinated and quick to flower.

Other species included *Paeonia anomala* and *P. wittmanniana*. These are closely related to *P. mlokosewitschii* and *P. veitchii* and share some of their growing qualities. The physical similarities of the four species are easy to see.

No woody peonies were listed.

Five species that are listed as easy to grow in North America are *Paeonia tenuifolia* 'Flore Plena', *P. mlokosewitschii, P. veitchii, P. anomala*, and *P. wittmanniana*.

EUROPE. The European growers had some similarities, but the milder climates of England and Ireland allow a wider range of species. Again *Paeonia tenuifolia* topped the list, with both *P. veitchii* and *P. mlokosewitschii* following closely. The next species, *P. emodi*, from the Himalayas, is generally too tender for many parts of the temperate United States. Again it is a distinc-

207

tive and easily recognized peony. The European list was also more extensive with a couple mentions of the woody peony, *Paeonia lutea* (as *P. ludlowii*), and a few people were very fond of *P. mascula*, *P. peregrina*, and *P. obovata* subsp. *japonica*.

European favorites are *Paeonia tenuifolia*, *P. mlokosewitschii*, *P. veitchii*, and *P. emodi*.

AUSTRALIA. The still milder climate of southern, more temperate Australia showed a preference for the species too tender for traditional cold climate peonies. The easiest species there was *Paeonia corsica* (as *P. cambessedesii*). This Mediterranean species is often damaged by late frosts as the early shoots and buds are emerging. This preference for mild-climate peonies is shown by other multiple mentions of the woody peony species *P. lutea* (as *P. ludlowii*), *P. suffruticosa* subsp. *ostii*, and the herbaceous *P. emodi* and *P. mascula* var. *russoi*. Other easy species included *P. officinalis*, *P. delavayi*, and *P. mlokosewitschii*. This is certainly the widest range including various woody and herbaceous species.

Australian easy peonies are *Paeonia corsica* (as *P. cambessedesii*), *P. lutea* (as *P. ludlowii*), *P. ostii*, *P. emodi*, and *P. mascula* var. *russoi*.

From these cross-continental lists, it is easy to see that some species accommodate well to growing in a wide range of climates and conditions AND perform well. In almost any temperate climate, beginners to peony species will enjoy *Paeony tenuifolia* and *P. mlokosewitschii*. In milder climates preference could be given to *P. emodi* and *P. lutea* (as *ludlowii*). These short lists make it abundantly clear that there are more choices in peonies for milder climates. While emphasis has been on growing peonies in more northerly areas, there are many excellent garden peonies for mild climates.

With this background, the beginning gardener is urged to try a few species that might be among the easier to grow. These are just guidelines and other species may be found growing in your area. Look around and ask questions. Perhaps your favorite nursery offers a species not mentioned on these lists. This probably suggests that it grows well for them and may work as well for you. New species and selections come into cultivation regularly. Growing peony species is an adventure in gardening, so be bold in selecting and growing more. Although a few species may be a challenge, there is great satisfaction in successful growth and bloom of these exotic treasures.

Peony Sources

Some species of the genus *Paeonia* are regularly available from many sources, but sources one year may not have the same seeds or plants available the next. The sources suggested below should be contacted before orders are placed to request a catalog or price list and to confirm availability and prices.

Seeds

Alpine Garden Society
AGS Centre
Avon Bank
Pershore
Worcestershire
United Kingdom WR10 3JP
Tel: +44 (0)1386 554 790
Fax: +44 (0)1386 554 801
Web: http://www.alpinegardensociety.org

Dr. Josef Halda
P.O. Box 110
501 01 Hradec Králové 2
Czech Republic
Web: http://www.paeon.de/h1/halda/fs_e.html

North American Rock Garden Society
P.O. Box 67
Millwood, New York 10546
Web: http://www.nargs.org

Phedar Nursery
42, Bunkers Hill
Romiley
Stockport
United Kingdom SK6 3DS
Tel: +44 (0)161 430 3772

Dr. Vlastimil Pilous
Jiraskova St. 396
543 71 Hostinné
Czech Republic
Fax: 00420 438 441373
Web: http://www.paeon.de/h1/pilous/fs_e.html

Thompson Morgan (USA)
P.O. Box 1308
Jackson, New Jersey 08527
Tel: 800-274-7333
Fax: 888-466-4769
Web: http://www.thompson-morgan.com/seeds/us/

Thompson & Morgan (UK)
Poplar Lane
Ipswich
Suffolk
United Kingdom IP8 3BU
Tel: +44 (0)1473 695200
Fax: +44 (0)1473 680 199
Web: http://www.thompson-morgan.com/seeds/uk/

Plants

Galen Burrell
P.O. Box 754
818 Sunset Lane
Ridgefield, Washington 98642

Heronswood Nursery
7530 NE 288th Street
Kingston, Washington 98346
Tel: 360-297-4172
Fax: 360-297-8321
Web: http://www.heronswood.com

Seneca Hill Perennials
3712 County Route 57
Oswego, New York 13126
Tel: 315-342-5915
Fax: 315-342-5573
Web: http://www.senecahill.com

Public Gardens

Bellevue Botanical Gardens, Bellevue, Washington, United States
Denver Botanical Gardens, Denver, Colorado, United States
Linda Hall Library, Kansas City, Missouri, United States
Royal Botanic Gardens, Kew, United Kingdom
Swarthmore College Arboretum, Swarthmore, Pennsylvania, United States

Websites

The World Wide Web and the Internet include some very interesting sites for peony information. The following organizational sites are worth exploring and many will lead to further good sources of information, seeds, and plants.

With Good Growing Info

Hollingsworth Nursery, http://www.hollingsworthpeonies.com
Nature's Promise, http://www.naturespromise.com/botany.html
La Pivoinerie D'Aoust, http://www.paeonia.com

Peony Societies

American Peony Society, http://www.americanpeonysociety.org/
Canadian Peony Society, http://www.peony.ca/
Heartland Peony Society, http://www.peonies.org/
Peony Society, http://www.peonysociety.org.uk/

Noncommercial Sites

Carsten Burkhardt, Germany, http://www.paeon.de/0site.html
Peter Faulbrueck, Germany, http://quadriga.net/index2.htm
Walter Good, Switzerland, http://www.paeonia.ch

Glossary

Acuminate Describes the ends of leaves tapering to a sharp point.

Attenuate Describes the base of leaves tapering to a point.

Bifurcate Forked, divided into two branches. See trifurcate

Biternate Doubly divided into three parts (see Figure 25, *P. daurica*). See ternate

Caniculate, Canaliculate Grooved.

Chartaceous Papery, thin; refers to leaf substance.

Circinate Coiled; arranged in a circle.

Coraliform Coral form; shaped like a coral.

Coriaceous Leathery.

Corolla A collective name for the petals of a flower. In *Paeonia*, the corolla consists of five or more petals.

Cuneate Wedge shaped, referring to the shape of the leaf base where it attaches to the petiole.

Digitate Literally "fingered," referring to a compound leaf composed of radiating leaflets.

Emarginate Having a notched edge particularly at the tip of the leaf.

Fasciculate Growing in clusters or bundles.

Floccose Having a woolly appearance or tufted with fine hairs.

Follicles The dried seedpod (fruit) derived from each carpel. These split along one side and display seed within. There are an equal number of carpels as follicles in the mature state.

Fusiform Spindle-shaped; elongate, widest in the middle and tapering at both ends.

Glabrous Smooth, hairless, bald.

Glaucous Gray-blue, bluish-green, or sea-green in color, associated with a smooth, waxy coating.

Gynoecium All the female reproductive parts of a flower. In peonies, the gynoecium consists of a single carpel (monocarpic) or multiple carpels (multicarpic).

Involucre A series of bracts or small leaves beneath a flower or inflorescence.

Pilose Downy; covered in fine, soft, long hairs. Compare pubescent

Pinnate Featherlike; in most plants, this refers to compound leaves with leaflets arranged on two sides of a central rachis or stalk.

Poculiform Cupped; cup-shaped.

Pubescent Having soft, short, fine hairs; velvety. Compare pilose

Scabrous Rough, covered in fine scales, projections, filelike.

Ternate Divided into three more or less equal leaflets. See biternate, triternate

Tomentose Woolly; covered in a coat of short, dense hairs.

Trifurcate Forked, divided into three branches.

Triternate Refers to compound leaves that are three times divided into three sets of leaflets (see Figure 37, *P. suffruticosa* subsp. *rockii*). See ternate

Vaginate Sheathed.

Villous Shaggy; covered in long straight hairs, not matted.

Bibliography

Albov, N. (1895): Prodromus Florae Colchicae. *Trudy Tiflissakago Botaniceskogo Sada*, 1, supplement 1: 14–15.

Anderson, E., and K. Sax (1936): Cytological Monograph of the American Species of *Tradescantia*. *Botanical Gazette* 97: 433–476.

Anderson, F. (1983): *German Book Illustrations through 1500. Herbals*. New York.

Anderson, G. (1880): A Monograph of the Genus *Paeonia. Transactions of the Linnean Society, London* 12: 248–290.

Andrews, H. (1804): *Paeonia suffruticosa. Botanist's Repository* 6: 373.

Andrews, H. (1807): *Paeonia daurica. Botanist's Repository* 7: 486.

Andrews, H. (1808): *Paeonia papaveracea. Botanist's Repository* 7: 463.

Arber, A. (1938): *Herbals, Their Origin and Evolution*, ed. 2. Cambridge.

Ascherson, P. F. A., and P. Graebner (1923): *Synopsis der Mitteleuropaischen Flora* 5 (2). Leipzig.

Aznavour, G. V. (1917): *Paeonia kavachensis. Magyar Bot. Lapok* 16: 7–8.

Bailey, I. W. (1951): The Use and Abuse of Anatomical Data in the Study of Phylogeny and Classification. *Phytomorphology* 1: 67–69.

Baillon, H. (1867): *Histoire des plantes*. 1: 476. Hachette, Paris.

Baker, J. G. (1884): *Paeonies. Gardeners' Chronicle*, ser. 3 (21): 732–780; (22): 9–10.

Barber, H. N. (1941): Evolution of the Genus *Paeonia. Nature* 148: 227.

Bartling, F. G. (1830): *Ordenes Naturales Plantarum*. Sumtibus Dieterichianis, Gottingae.

Bauhin, C. (1623): *Pinax Theatri botanici sive Index in Theophrasti, Dioscoridis, Plinii et botanicorum*. Basel.

Bentham, G., and J. D. Hooker (1862): *Genera Plantarum* 1: 1–15. L. Reeve and Company, London.

Besler, B. (1613): *Hortus Eystettensis*. Nuremberg.

Boissier, P. E. (1838): *Elenchus Plantarum novarum*. Geneva.

Boissier, P. E. (1839–1845): *Voyage botanique dans le Midi de l'Espagne* 2 (14), t. 3: 714. Paris.

Boissier, P. E. (1867): *Flora Orientalis* 1: 97–98. Geneva.

Boissier, P. E., and G. F. Reuter (1842): Diagnoses Plantarum novarum Hispanicarum 4. *Biblioth. Univ. Geneve*, new ser. 38: 196.

Boyd, J., ed. (1928): *Peonies; the Manual of the American Peony Society.* Robbinsdale, Minnesota.

Bretschneider, E. (1898): *History of European Botanical Discoveries in China,* 1. London.

Briquet, J. (1910): *Prodrome de la Flore Corse* 1. Geneva and Basel.

Brouland, M. (1935): Recherches sur l'anatomie floral des Ranunculacees. *Le Botaniste* 27: 1–278.

Broussalis, P. (1978): The Genus *Paeonia* in Greece. *H Fidis* 14: 10–14, 38–39.

Bruehl, P. (1896): *Paeonia moutan. Annals of the Royal Botanic Garden, Calcutta* 5: 114–115, t. 126.

Bunge, A. von (1833): Enumeratio Plantarum quas in China Boreali Collegit 3. *Mémoires de l'Académie Impériale des Sciences de St.-Petersbourg* 2: 77.

Busch, N. A. (1901–1903): *Paeonia. Flora Caucasica Critica* 3. Tartu, Estonia.

Cambessedes, J. (1827): Enumeratio Plantarum quas in Insulis Balearibus collegit 33. *Mem. Mus. Hist. Nat. Paris* 14: 205.

Camp, W. H., and M. M. Hubbard (1963): Vascular Supply and Structure of the Ovule and Aril in Peony and of the Aril in Nutmeg. *American Journal of Botany* 50: 174–178.

Carniel, K. (1967): Über die Embryobildung in der Gattung *Paeonia. Österreichische botanische Zeitschrift* 114: 4–19.

Caruel, T. (1860): *Prodromo della Flora Toscana* 19–20. Florence.

Cave, M. S., H. J. Arnott, and S. A. Cook (1961): Embryogeny in the California Peonies with Reference to Their Taxonomic Positions. *American Journal of Botany* 48: 397–404.

Chabert, A. (1889): *Paeonia algeriensis. Bulletin de la Société botanique de France* 36: 18–19.

Clusius, C. (1583): *Rariorum Aliquot Stirpium per Pannoniam, Austriam, et Vicinas Quasdam Provincias Observatarum Historia.* 401–402. Antwerp.

Clusius, C. (1601): *Rariorum Plantarum Historia.* 279–281. Antwerp.

Corner, E. J. (1946): Centrifugal Stamens. *Journal of the Arnold Arboretum* 27: 423–437.

Corner, E. J. (1953): The Durian Theory Extended I. *Phytomorphology* 3: 465–476.

Corner, E. J. (1954): The Durian Theory Extended II. The Arillate Fruit and the Compound Leaf. *Phytomorphology* 4: 152–165.

Cosson, E. St. Ch. (1850): *Notes sur quelques plantes de France* 2: 49. Paris.

Cosson, E. St. Ch. (1887): *Compendium Florae Atlanticae* 2: 52–55. Paris.

Creutzburg, N. (1963): Die Palaogeographische Entwicklung der Insel Kreta von Miozan bus zur Gegenwart. *Kritische Kronika* 15: 336–344.

Creutzburg, N. (1966): Die Sudaigaische Inselbrucke, Bau und Geologische Vergangenheit. *Erdkunde* 20: 20–30.

Cronquist, A. (1968): *The Evolution and Classification of Flowering Plants.* Boston, Houghton Mifflin.

Cronquist, A. (1981): *An Integrated System of Classification of Flowering Plants.* New York.

Cullen, J., and V. H. Heywood (1964a): Notes on the European Species of *Paeonia. Feddes Repertorium* 69: 32–35.

Cullen, J., and V. H. Heywood (1964b): *Paeonia.* In Tutin, T. G., et al., *Flora Europaea.* Cambridge University Press. 1: 243–244.

Cupani, F. (1696): *Hortus Catholicus.* Palermo.

Cupani, F. (1713): *Pamphyton Siculum.* Palermo.

Dark, S. O. S. (1936): Meiosis in Diploid and Tetraploid *Paeonia* Species. *Journ. Genetics* 32: 353.

Davis, P. H., and J. Cullen (1965): *Paeonia*. In Davis, P. H., ed., *Flora of Turkey*. Edinburgh University Press. 1: 204–206.

De Candolle, Augustin P. (1817): *Regni Vegetabilis Systema Naturale* 1: 386–394.

De Candolle, Augustin P. (1824): *Prodromus Systematis Naturalis Regni Vegetabilis* 1: 65–66.

Dickison, W. C. (1967): Comparative Morphological Studies in Dilleniaceae. *Journal of the Arnold Arboretum* 48: 1–29.

Dioscorides, P. (1829): *De Materia Medica* 1: 486–487. Leipzig.

Eames, A. J. (1961): *Morphology of the Angiosperms*. McGraw Hill, New York.

Engler, A., and E. Gilg (1924): *Syllabus Pflanzenfamilien*, ed. 9. W. Engelmann, Leipzig.

Ezelarab, G. E., and K. J. Dormer (1963): The Organization of the Primary Vascular System in Ranunculaceae. *Annals of Botany* 27: 23–38.

Fang, W. P. (1958): Notes on Chinese Peonies. *Acta Phytotaxonomica Sinica* 7 (4): 297–323.

Farrer, R. J. (1914): Explorations in China 2. In Kansu. *Gardeners' Chronicle*, ser. 3 (56): 213.

Farrer, R. J. (1916): *Paeonia moutan. Journal of the Royal Horticultural Society* 42: 88.

Farrer, R. J. (1917): *On the Eaves of the World* 1: 110–112.

Fedtschenko, B. A. (1904): Flora Zapadnovo Tjan-Shana 1: 103–105. *Acta Horti Petropolitani* 23: 351.

Finet, A. E., and F. Gagnepain (1905): Contributions à la Flore de l'Asie Orientale. *Bulletin de la Société botanique de France* 51: 523–527.

Forrest, G. (1920): *Paeonia delavayi. Gardeners' Chronicle* 68 (3): 97–98.

Fournier, P. (1948): *Le Livre des plantes medicinales et veneneuses de France* 3: 237–239. Paris.

Franchet, A. (1886): Plantae Yunnanenses. XXX. *Paeonia. Bulletin de la Société botanique de France* 33: 382–383.

Fritsch, C., Jr. (1899): Beitrage zur Flora der Balkanhalbinsel 4: 84–85. *Verhandlungen der Kayserlich-Königlichen Zoologisch-Botanischen Gesellschaft in Wien* 49: 240–242.

Fuchs, L. (1542): *De Historia Stirpium* (Treatise on herbs). Basel.

Fuchs, L. (1543): *New Kreuterbuch*. Basel.

Gottsberger, G. (1977): Some Aspects of Beetle Pollination in the Evolution of Flowering Plants. *Plant Systematics and Evolution, Supplement* 1: 211–226.

Greuter, W. (1977): Chorological Additions to the Greek Flora, 1. *Candollea* 32: 21–49.

Greuter, W. (1979): The Origins and Evolution of Island Floras as Exemplified by the Aegean Archipelago. In Bramwell, D., ed., *Plants and Islands*. London: Academic Press. 87–106.

Grossheim, A. A. (1930): *Flora Kavkaza* 2: 90–92. Tiflis.

Halda, J. (1997): Systematic Treatment of the Genus *Paeonia* L. with Some Nomenclatoric Changes. *Acta Musei Richnoviensis* 4 (2): 25–32.

Halda, J. (1998): Notes on the Observations upon the Structure of the *Paeonia* Seeds, Fruits and Roots. *Acta Musei Richnoviensis* 6 (3): 1–11.

Halda, J. (1999): New Descriptions and Combinations. *Acta Musei Richnoviensis* 6 (3): 234.

Handel-Mazzetti, H. (1931): *Symbolae Sinicae* 7: 265–266. Vienna.

Handel-Mazzetti, H. (1939): Plantae Sinenses. XXX. *Paeonia. Acta Horti Gothoburg* 13: 37–40.

Hao, H. D., M. H. Zang, and C. Fan (1992): *An Introduction to Heze Peony of China*. Heze, China: Heze Peony Research Institute.

Haw, S. G. (1985): Mudan: the King of Flowers. *The Garden* 110 (4): 154–159.

Haw, S. G. (1986): A Problem of Peonies. *The Garden* 111 (7): 326–328.

Haw, S. G., and L. A. Lauener (1990): A Review of the Intraspecific Taxa of *Paeonia suffruticosa* Andrews. *Edinburgh Journal of Botany* 47 (3): 273–281.

Haworth-Booth, M. (1963): *The Moutan or Tree Peony.* London: Constable.

Hiepko, P. (1965): Das zentrifugale Androecium der Paeoniaceae. *Berichte der Deutschen botanischen Gesellschaft* 77: 427.

Hong, T., J. X. Zhang, J. J. Li, W. Z. Zhao, and M. R. Li (1992): Study of the Chinese Wild Woody Peonies. *Bulletin of Botanical Research, Harbin* 12: 223–224.

Hooker, J. D. (1872): *Flora of British India* 1: 30. London.

Hooker, J. D. (1882): *Paeonia wittmanniana. Botanical Magazine, Tokyo,* 108: 6645.

Hooker, J. D. (1901): *Paeonia lutea. Botanical Magazine, Tokyo,* 127: 7788.

Hooker, W. J. (1829): *Flora Boreali-Americana* 1: 27. London.

Hutchinson, J. (1959): *The Families of Flowering Plants,* 2nd ed. Oxford, Clarendon Press.

Huth, E. (1891): Monographie der Gattung *Paeonia. Botanische Jahrbücher* 14: 258–276.

Hylander, N. (1938): Om Bondpionens Uppkomst och Vetenskapliga namn. *Lustgarden* 18–19: 69–76.

Jahandiez, E., and R. Maire (1932): *Catalogue des Plantes du Maroc* 2: 239–240. Alger.

Janchen, E. (1949): Die Systematische Gliederung der Ranunculaceen und Berberidaceen. *Denkschriften der Akademie der Wissenschaften, Wien,* 108: 1–82.

Jordan, A., and J. Foureau (1903): *Icones ad Floram Europae novo Fundamento instaurandum spectantes* 2: 37–38, tt. 318–323. Paris.

Keefe, J. M., and F. M. Maynard (1978): Wood Anatomy and Phylogeny of *Paeonia* Section *Moutan. Journal of the Arnold Arboretum* 59: 274.

Kemularia-Nathadze, L. M. (1961): Kavkazskije Predstaviteli Roda *Paeonia* L. (Caucasian representatives of the genus *Paeonia* L.). Not. Syst. Geog. Inst. Bot. Tbiliss, *Trudy Tbilisi Botanical Institute* 21: 3–51.

Komarov, V. L. (1921): Plantae Novae Chinenses. *Notulae Syst. Herb. Horti Petrop.* 2: 5–8.

Komarov, V. L., ed. (1937): *Flora of the USSR* 7. Leningrad

Kroeber, L. (1937): *Das Neuzeitliche Krauterbuch,* ed. 3, 1: 267–270. Stuttgart.

Krylov, P. N. (1901): *Flora Altaja* 1:46. Tomsk.

Krylov, P. N. (1931): *Flora Sibirae Occidentalis* 5: 116–118. Tomsk.

Kumazawa, M. (1935): The Structure and Affinities of *Paeonia. Botanical Magazine, Tokyo* 49: 306–315.

Langlet, O. F. I. (1927): Beitrage zur Zytologie der Ranunculazeen. *Svensk Botanisk Tidskrift* 21: 1–17.

Lauener, L. A. (1989): The Mudan and the Scottish Connection. *Sine* (Bulletin of the Scotland-China Association), pp. 7–9.

Ledebour, C. F., et al. (1830): *Flora Altaica* 2: 276–279. Berlin.

Le Grand, A. (1899): *Paeonia russi* var. *reverchoni. Bull. Assoc. Franc. Bot.* 2 (15):62.

Lemesle, R. (1955): Contribution à l'Étude de quelques familles de Dicotyledones considerées comme primitives. *Phytomorphology* 5: 11–45.

Leppik, E. E. (1964): Floral Evolution in the Ranunculaceae. *Iowa State Journal of Science* 39: 1–101.

Léveillé, A. A. H. (1915): *Paeonia mairei. Bull. Acad. Internat. Geographie Bot.,* Le Mans 25:42.

Lindley, J. (1839): *Paeonia brownii. Botanical Register* 25: 30.

Lindley, J. (1846): *Paeonia wittmanniana. Botanical Register* 32: 9.

Linnaeus, C. (1737, transl. 1938): Critica Botanica. 124. *Ray Society Publication.* London. (1753)

l'Obel, M. de (1581): *Plantarum seu stirpium icones.* Antwerp.

Lomakin, A. A. (1897): De Paeoniis Novis in Caucaso Crescentibus. *Trudy Tiflissakago Botaniceskogo Sada* 2: 280.

Lotsy, J. P. (1911): *Vorträge über otanische Stammengeschichte* 3. Fischer, Jena.

Lynch, R. I. (1890): A New Classification of the Genus *Paeonia*. *Journal of the Royal Horticultural Society* 12: 428.

Lynch, R. I. (1909): *Paeonia veitchii. Gardeners' Chronicle*, ser. 3: 46.

Makino, T. (1898): *Paeonia obovata* Maxim. var. *japonica* Makino. *Botanical Magazine, Tokyo*, 12: 302.

Maleev, V. P. (1937): Zametka o Gibridnom Peone iz Krima. *Sovietskaja Bot.* 1937 (1): 128–130.

Mandl, K. (1921–1922): *Paeonia vernalis. Botanikai Közlemenyek* 19: 90.

Marzell, H. (1976): *Worterbuch der deutschen Pflanzennamen* 3: 501–523. Stuttgart.

Mattioli, P. A. (1562): *Herbarz Jinak Bylinarz na Czeskou Rzecz od Thaddease z Hajku prze-lozeny*, pp. 274–275. Prague.

Mattioli, P. A. (1565): *Commentarii in sex libros Pedacii Dioscoridis* (Commentary on the Six Books of Pedanios Dioscorides) 2. Venice.

Maximowicz, C. J. (1859): Primitiae Florae Amurensis. *Mémoires de l'Académie impériale des Sciences de St.-Petersbourg* 9.

Melchior, H., and E. Werdermann (1954): A. *Engler's Syllabus der Pflanzenfamilien*, 12th ed. Berlin.

Melville, R. (1983): The Affinity of *Paeonia* and a Second Genus of Paeoniaceae. *Kew Bulletin* 38: 87–105.

Mioni, E. (1959): Un Ignorato Dioscoride Miniato. Il Cordice Greco 194 del Seminario di Padova. In Barzon, A., ed., *Libri e Stampatori in Padova. Miscellanea di Studi Storici in Onore di Mons. C. Bellini.* Padova. 345: 376.

Moore, S. L. M. (1879): *Paeonia oreogeton. Journal of the Linnean Society, London, Botany* 17: 376–377.

Moris, G. G. (1837): *Flora Sardoa* 1: 64. Turin.

Moss, C. E. (1920): *The Cambridge British Flora* 3: 155–156. Cambridge.

Opsomer, C., W. T. Stearn, and I. Roberts (1984): *Livre des Simples Medecines: Codex Bruxellensis.* English translation with commentaries. Antwerp.

Pacht, O. (1975): Die früheste abendlandische Kopie des Illustrationen des Wiener Dioskurides. *Zeitschrift für Kunstgeschichte* 37: 201–214.

Page, Martin (1997): *The Gardener's Guide to Growing Peonies.* Timber Press. Portland, Oregon, United States.

Pallas, P. S. (1776): *Reise durch verschiedene Provinzen des russischen Reichs* 3: 286. St. Petersburg.

Pallas, P. S. (1788): *Flora Rossica* 1 (2): 92–95. St. Petersburg.

Pan, K. Y. (1979): *Paeonia.* In *Flora Reipublicae Popularis Sinicae.* Beijing: Science Press. 27: 37–59.

Papamichael, A. J. (1975): *Birth and Plant Symbolism. Symbolic and Magical Uses of Plants in Connection with Birth in Modern Greece.* Athens.

Partridge, E. (1966): *Origins, a Short Etymological Dictionary of Modern English.* London.

Pliny the Elder (1601): *The Historie of the World.* Trans. Philemon Holland. London.

Prantl, K. A. (1888): *Ranunculaceae.* In Engler and Prantl, *Die natürlichen Pflanzenfamilien.* Berlin. 3 (2): 43–66.

Presl, K. B. (1822): *Paeonia flavescens* J. S. & K. B. Presl. In *Deliciae Pragenses, Historia naturalem spectantes*. Prague. 1: 5.

Rechinger, K. H. (1951): Phytogeographia Aegea. *Denkschriften der Akademie der Wissenschaften, Wien, Math.-Nat*. 105 (2): 1–208.

Rehder, A. (1920): *Paeonia suffruticosa* var. *spontanea*. *Journal of the Arnold Arboretum* 1: 193–194.

Rehder, A., and C. E. Kobuski (1933): An Enumeration of the Herbaceous Plants Collected by J. F. Rock. *Journal of the Arnold Arboretum* 14: 10.

Rehder, A., and E. H. Wilson. (1913): *Plantae Wilsonianae*, ed. C. S. Sargent 1: 318. Cambridge, Massachusetts

Rochel, A. (1828): *Plantae Banatus Rariores* 48: 11–12. Budapest.

Rogers, A. (1995): *Peonies*. Timber Press, Portland, Oregon.

Rolland, E. (1896): *Flore populaire* 1: 119–128. Paris.

Rouy, G., and J. Foucaud (1893): *Flore de France* 1: 143. Asnieres and Rochefort.

Runemark, H. (1971): Distribution Patterns in the Aegean. In Davis, P. H., et al., eds., *Plant Life of Southwest Asia*. *Botanical Society of Edinburgh*. 3–12.

Ruprecht, F. J. (1869): *Flora Caucasica. Mémoires de l'Académie Impériale des Sciences de St.-Petersbourg* 7 (15): 2.

Sabine, J., and J. Lindley (1824): *Paeonia cretica*. *Botanical Register* 10: 819.

Saint-Lager, J. B. (1884): Recherches historiques sur les mots "Plantes Males" et "Plantes Femelles." *Annales de la Société botanique de Lyon* 11 (1883): 1–48.

Saunders, A. P., and G. L. Stebbins (1938): Cytogenetic Studies in *Paeonia* 1. *Genetics* 23: 65–82.

Saunders, S. (1934): A Portfolio of Peony Species. *National Horticulture Magazine* (Washington, D.C.) 13: 213.

Sawada, M. (1971): Floral Vascularization of *Paeonia japonica* with Some Consideration on Systematic Position of Paeoniaceae. *Botanical Magazine, Tokyo*, 84: 51–60.

Schipczinski, N. V. (1921): Kratkij Obzor Roda *Paeonia*. *Notulae systematicae ex herbario horti botanici petropolitanae* 2: 41.

Schipczinski, N. V., and V. L. Komarov (1937): *Paeonia*. In Komarov, V. L., ed., *Flora of the USSR*. Leningrad. 7: 24–35.

Smrz, Oskar (1925): *Pivonky a jak se Pestuji* (Peonies and how to grow them). Pardubice, Czech Republic.

Sopova, M. (1971): The Cytological Study of Two *Paeonia* Species from Macedonia. *Fragmenta Balcanica Musei Macedoni Scientiarum naturalium* 8 (16): 137–142.

Sprague, T. A., and E. Nelmes (1931): The Herbal of Leonhart Fuchs. *Journal of the Linnean Society, London, Botany* 47: 545–642.

Stannard, J. (1969): P. A. Mattioli: Sixteenth-Century Commentator on Dioscorides. University of Kansas Libraries. *Bibliographical Contributions* 7: 58–81.

Stannard, J. (1971): Byzantine Botanical Lexicography. *Episteme* 5: 168–187.

Stapf, O. (1916): *Paeonia willmottiae*. *Botanical Magazine, Tokyo*, 142: 8667.

Stapf, O. (1918): *Paeonia peregrina*. *Botanical Magazine, Tokyo*, 144: 8742.

Stapf, O. (1931): *Paeonia tomentosa*. *Botanical Magazine, Tokyo*, 155: 9249.

Stearn, W. T. (1941): *Paeonia rhodia*, the Wild Paeony of Rhodes. *Gardeners' Chronicle*, ser. 3 (110): 158–160.

Stearn, W. T. (1976): From Theophrastus and Dioscorides to Sibthorp and Smith: the Background and Origin of the *Flora Graeca*. *Journal of the Linnean Society, London, Biology* 8: 285–298.

Stearn, W. T. (1979): The Historical Background to the Illustrations of the "Herbarium Apulei" and "Herbolario volgare." In Edizioni il Polifilo facsimile, *Herbarium Apulei 1481, Herbolario volgare*. Milan. 1522 1: vii–xxi.

Stearn, W. T., and P. H. Davis (1984): *Peonies of Greece: A Taxonomic and Historical Survey of the Genus* Paeonia *in Greece*. Goulandris Natural History Museum, Kifissia, Greece.

Stebbins, G. L. (1938): Cytogenetic Studies in *Paeonia* 2. *Genetics* 23: 83.

Stebbins, G. L. (1938): The American Species of *Paeonia. Madrono* 4: 252.

Stebbins, G. L. (1939): Notes on Some Systematic Relationships in the Genus *Paeonia. University of California Publications in Botany* 19 (7): 245–266.

Stebbins, G. L., and S. Ellerton (1939): Structural Hybridity in *P. californica* and *P. brownii. Journal of Genetics* 38: 1.

Stern, F. C. (1931): Paeony Species. *Journal of Royal Horticultural Society* 56: 71–77.

Stern, F. C. (1939): The Moutan Paeony. *Journal of the Royal Horticultural Society* 64: 550.

Stern, F. C. (1943): Genus *Paeonia. Journal of the Royal Horticultural Society* 68: 124.

Stern, F. C. (1946): *A Study of the Genus* Paeonia. London.

Stern, F. C. (1959): *Paeonia suffruticosa* Rock's Variety. *Journal of the Royal Horticultural Society* 84: 366.

Steven, C. von (1848): *Paeonia wittmanniana. Bulletin de la Société Imperiale des Naturalistes de Moscow* 21 (3): 275.

Takeda, H. (1910): *Paeonia japonica. Gardeners' Chronicle* 3 (48): 366.

Tamura, M. (1963): Morphology, Ecology and Phylogeny of the Ranunculaceae. *Sci. Rep. Osaka Univ.* 11:115-126.

Tamura, M. (1972): Morphology and Phyletic Relations of Glaucidiaceae. *Botanical Magazine, Tokyo,* 85: 29–41.

Tausch, I. F. (1828): Bemerkungen über einige Arten der Gattung *Paeonia. Flora* (Regensburg) 11: 81–89.

Theophrastus (1916): *Enquiry into Plants.* Trans. A. F. Hort. London. 2: 257.

Thiébaut, J. (1936): Flore Libano-Syrienne, 1, p. 37. Reprinted in *Mémoires présente à l'Institut d'Égypte,* p. 31.

Thoms, H., ed. (1929): *Handbuch der praktischen und wissenschaftlichen Pharmazie* 5 (1): 819–822. Berlin and Vienna.

Thorne, R. F. (1968): Synopsis of a Putatively Phylogenetic Classification of the Flowering Plants. *Aliso* 6 (4): 57–66.

Torrey, J., and A. Gray (1838): *Flora of North America.* 2 vols. Reprint. 1: 40.

Tzanoudakis, D. M. (1977): *Cytotaxonomic Study of the Genus* Paeonia *in Greece* (in Greek). Patras, Greece.

Tzanoudakis, D. M. (1983): Karyotypes of Four *Paeonia* Species from Greece. *Nordic Journal of Botany* 3: 307–318.

Uspenskaja, M. S. (1987): Dopolnenie k Sisteme Roda *Paeonia* L. *Byulleten Moskovskogo Obshchestva Ispytatelei Prirody, Biology,* 92 (3): 79–85.

Walters, J. L. (1962): Megasporogenesis and Gametophyte Selection in *Paeonia californica. American Journal of Botany* 49: 287–794.

Wellmann, M. (1889): Sextius Niger. Eine Quellenuntersuchung zu Dioscorides. *Hermes* 24: 520–569.

Wellmann, M., ed. (1906): *Pedanii discuridis de Materia Medica.* Berlin: Weidmann.

Willkomm, H. M. (1883): *Illustrationes Florae Hispanicae Insularumque Balearium* 1: 104.

Wister, J. C., ed. (1962): *The Peonies.* American Horticultural Society, Washington, D.C.

Worsdell, W. C. (1908): The Affinities of *Paeonia. Journal of Botany, London* 46: 114–116.

Wren, R. C. (1968): *Potter's New Cyclopaedia of Botanical Drugs and Preparations,* 8th ed.

Wyman, D. (1936): Tree Peonies. *Arnoldia* 29: 25–32.

Xin, J., ed. (1986): *The Peony in Luoyang.* Beijing: China Pictorial.

Yakovlev, M. S., and M. D. Yoffe (1957): On Some Peculiar Features in the Embryology of *Paeonia* L. *Phytomorphology* 7: 74–82.

Yu, C., S. Li, and J. Zhou (1987): Karyotype Analysis of *Paeonia suffruticosa* var. *papaveracea* and *P. suffruticosa* var. *spontanea. Acta Botanica Boreo-Occidentale Sinica* 7 (1): 12–16.

General Index

Index of Peony Species

Scientific names are given without regard to taxonomic level except for recognized valid species. Page references will clarify. Names with similar spelling will be found under a single heading, that is, *P. russoi* includes *P. russi* and *P. russii*. Some names will be found only in this index, for example, *P. smouthii*. Boldface page numbers indicate main species entries. Italic page numbers indicate illustrations.

226

INDEX OF PEONY SPECIES